**Tom**

**Ross**

*methuen* | drama

LONDON • NEW YORK • OXFORD • NEW DELHI • SYDNEY

METHUEN DRAMA
Bloomsbury Publishing Plc
50 Bedford Square, London, WC1B 3DP, UK
1385 Broadway, New York, NY 10018, USA

BLOOMSBURY, METHUEN DRAMA and the Methuen Drama logo are
trademarks of Bloomsbury Publishing Plc

First published in Great Britain 2019

Cover design by Ben Anslow
Cover images: *A Girl with a Flower in Her Hair*, Pietro Rotari (1762)
(© Artokoloro Quint Lox Limited / Alamy),
Texture © Digital Yard Sale, Ornaments © freepik

A catalogue record for this book is available from the British Library.

ISBN: PB: 978-1-3501-3367-9
ePDF: 978-1-3501-3368-6
eBook: 978-1-3501-3369-3

Series: Modern Plays

Typeset by Mark Heslington Ltd, Scarborough, North Yorkshire
Printed and bound in Great Britain

To find out more about our authors and books visit
www.bloomsbury.com and sign up for our newsletters.

# Introduction

I think my first experience of Henry Fielding's *Tom Jones* was the wonderful film by Tony Richardson, starring the great Albert Finney. It used to be on regularly on a Sunday afternoon and I would always find myself watching it, and I had not the tiniest of inklings back then how much this madcap tale would end up changing my life.

It all started when I was cast in a stage version of *Tom Jones* back in the mid-nineties, where I played Squire Weston and Mr Thwackam in an extensive West Country tour. It was written and directed by a chap called Michael Barry, to whom I will always be grateful for igniting a passion in me for this bawdy romp and for introducing me to two characters that have stayed with me for over twenty years. I seem to remember his adaptation was pretty good, but I also remember thinking I could do better. Arrogant I know, especially when at that point I hadn't really written anything at all, but two years later I found myself trapped in a hotel room in the middle of Saudi Arabia, with nothing to amuse me but a copy of Henry Fielding's foot-thick tome, and that was when I finally knuckled down and got on with it. I didn't even have a laptop, I had to write it out longhand, but I started to enjoy the process and eventually I ended up with something that I didn't think was that bad. So much so that, when I returned to the UK, I got a bunch of actors together and we took it up to the Edinburgh Fringe.

I learnt a lot that year from doing the Fringe – my first. The main lesson being that instead of bringing up a full-length play and a large cast one should, as I think Steve Coogan once said, save yourself the grief and put your money in a bucket and set fire to it. Having said that it was a very worthwhile experience and I would do it again in an instant, for it taught me more than any convoluted college course could ever do and allowed me to find out if I was any good – because that's what every writer has to find out, isn't it?

I remember one night Tamsin, who was playing Sophia, noted that I was not my usually composed self. I am one of these annoying people who doesn't get nervous before I go on stage, but this particular night I was on edge and she had never seen me like it before. It was because we had *The Scotsman* in, this was going to be my first Edinburgh review, and I felt my entire future lay in the hands of someone called Tilly or Totty or something like that.

There was no getting away from it, I had written the piece, I had directed it, I was acting in it and, if it got a bad review, it was down to me. Well, thankfully, it didn't get a bad review. In fact they quite liked it, especially the writing, and at that moment a whole new world of opportunities opened up for me, and you can blame Tilly or Totty or whoever she was for creating the megalomaniac you see before you today.

So, there you have it, *Tom Jones* was my first, and I am sure you can imagine how chuffed I am to finally see it in print. I know, you don't have to point it out, it is an adaptation and I didn't have to do any of the heavy lifting. I am standing firmly on the broad shoulders of a literary genius. The wit, the language, the observations of the human condition, it was already there upon the page and all I had to do was bugger about with it a bit. Henry Fielding was undoubtedly a man of infinite intellect, humour and empathy and, more importantly, someone who knew the value of a good muff gag, and I can only hope that through my humble efforts he will find a wider audience, and many more people will join me in lifting the occasional glass or two to his name.

*Tom Jones* was first performed at Edinburgh Fringe in 2001 where the cast included Ross Ericson, Peter Ferdinando, Tamsin Skan and Shirley Newbury. It was revived in 2011 at The Lion and Unicorn Theatre, Kentish Town, where the cast included Ross Ericson, Edward Kingham, Simon Grieves, Ben Bellamy, Sarah Kelly, Kate Mounce, Stephanie Martin and Clare Walsh.

The current production is a co-production between Red Dragonfly Productions, Grist To The Mill Productions and The Rotunda Theatre.

## Cast and Creatives

| | |
|---|---|
| Tom Jones | **Victor Itang** |
| Sophia | **Ainsleigh Barber** |
| Fielding/Allworthy | **Ellis J. Wells** |
| Blifil/Mr Fitzpatrick/Lord Fellamar | **Sunjay Midda** |
| Mrs Weston/Landlady/Lady Bellaston | **Michelle Lee** |
| Thwackam/Weston/Northerton | **Ross Ericson** |
| Molly/Mrs Fitzpatrick | **Harriet Sharmini Smithers** |
| Mrs Honour/Mrs Waters | **Michelle Yim** |

| | |
|---|---|
| *Writer/Director* | Ross Ericson |
| *Producer* | Michelle Yim |
| *Stage Manager* | Alan Law |
| *Costume* | Elizabeth Cooke |
| *Set, Lighting and Sound Design* | The Millers |

### Ross Ericson – Weston/Thwackam/Northerton/ Writer/Director

Ross has been acting since the mid-1990s and has appeared most recently as Lennie in *Of Mice and Men* (Lighthouse, Poole), a Corner man/Bailiff in *Sucker Punch* (Royal Court, London), Ben in *The Dumb Waiter* (The Mill Theatre, Guildford), Number 4 in *Fewer Emergencies* (The Print Room, London), Ned in *Parlour Song* (Cockpit Theatre, London), Jake in *27 Wagons Full of Cotton* (Riverside Studios, London) and The Stage Manager in *Our Town* (Apollo Theatre Company, Touring). He is currently touring internationally with his critically acclaimed solo shows *The Unknown Soldier* and *Gratiano*. Among his writing credits are *Casualties, The Unknown Soldier* and *Gratiano*, all published by Methuen Drama, *Punchline, Life, The Autumn of Han, DiaoChan, The Empress and Me, An Evening With Miss Wong*, and a stage adaptation from the Chinese classic *Journey To The West* called *Monkey and The White Bone Demon*. He also has numerous directing credits and is the artistic director of Grist To The Mill Productions and joint artistic director of Rotunda Theatre.

### Michelle Yim – Mrs Honour/Mrs Waters/Producer

Graduated from ALRA. Her recent theatre includes: *From Shore to Shore* (Touring), *DiaoChan* (Red Dragonfly, Touring), *Arrivals* (NI Tour) and *The King and I* (Theatre at the Mill, NI). She is currently touring internationally with her critically acclaimed solo shows *An Evening with Miss Wong* and *The Empress and Me* and has appeared in numerous short films and in small roles on TV – notably in *Strangers, Sherlock* and *Blue Murder*. She works extensively as a voiceover artist in English, Cantonese and Mandarin and has a number of producing and directing credits to her name. Michelle has also worked extensively in the field of audience development and is the Artistic Director of Red Dragonfly Productions and Joint Artistic Director of Rotunda Theatre.

### Ainsleigh Barber – Sophia

Ainsleigh graduated from Aberystwyth University in Drama, Theatre and Performance studies in 2013. Now based in Cardiff, her film and stage credits include *Offworld*, a SciFi film that was filmed entirely in Wales, and The Sherman Player's *Dracula*. Most recently she toured Saudi Arabia as Baby Bop in *Barney Live: World Tour* and worked on BBC's *His Dark Materials*. When not performing, she plays Video/Board-games and loves Japanese culture and eating Mochi and Sushi.

## Victor Itang – Tom

Victor is a Filipino actor who trained at East 15 acting school and has been working professionally ever since graduating in 2016. Some of his theatre work includes *Comedy of Errors* (RSC Dell), *Karlstad* (The Courtyard) and *Bibs, Boats, Borders and Bastards* (the Cockpit). When he isn't glued to the TV or visiting the theatres and cinemas – all for research, of course – Victor spends his time working out, travelling and socialising.

## Sunjay Midda – Blifil/Mr Fitzpatrick/Lord Fellamar

Within a month of Sunjay graduating with his level 3 diploma in Acting & Theatre studies he landed the role of 'Shak' in BBC's *Doctors* and has never looked back. He has been playing the semi-regular role to this day, but is relishing the opportunity of being back on stage and working alongside the Red Dragonfly team hoping to 'open your world of imagination'.

## Michelle Lee – Mrs Weston/Landlady/Lady Bellaston

Michelle is a British Malaysian Chinese dancer, singer, musician and actor who started performing professionally at the age of 12. She trained at Mountview Theatre School, Birmingham University and Bush Davies. Her West End credits include *Miss Saigon* and *Hey Mr Producer!*, and recent theatre includes *Little Potatoes* (Edinburgh Fringe) and *The Red Court* (Bath Fringe). Her extensive film and TV credits include *Hummingbird, London Road, Bridget Jones: Edge of Reason, Rogue Trader, Strangers, The Bill* and *Powers*.

## Ellis J. Wells – Henry Fielding/Allworthy

Ellis J. Wells was born in Bristol and made his acting debut at Bristol Grammar School in a production of Bertolt Brecht's *Fear and Misery of the Third Reich*. He attended university in Iowa, where he was nominated for Best Actor at KCACTF for his performance as Puck in *A Midsummer Night's Dream*. His theatre credits include Col. Pickering in *Pygmalion* (Tour of Italy), Dr Seward in *Dracula*, Dr Watson in *The Accidental Adventures of Sherlock Holmes*, the title role in *Richard III*, Cardinal Richelieu in *The Three Musketeers*, Caliban in *The Tempest*, Bob Cratchit in *A Christmas Carol* and Matt in the one-man show *Facehugger*.

## Harriet Sharmini Smithers – Molly/Mrs Fitzpatrick

Harriet trained at University of Birmingham in Drama and Theatre arts and graduated in 2014. Her credits include the films *Horndog* and *AOP Vs The World,* the touring theatre productions of *Classified* and *Taking Flight,* and immersive theatre productions of *Father Christmas at the Hall* and *Lost Lagoon*. She has also worked as a voice-over artist and appeared in several commercials, notably for Lebara and Legal and General.

## Alan Law – Stage Manager

Allan studied Drama with David Johnson and Emma Stafford in Manchester. His stage credits include *The Autumn Of Han* (Red Dragonfly Productions, Touring) and *Somme Men* (Tale Spin Theatre Co, Liverpool). His has appeared in the film *Empire Of Silver* and was a voice actor on the award winning BBC animation/radio drama *Quake*.

## Elizabeth Cooke – Costumes

Elizabeth is a costumer with over five years experience working on theatre, dance and acrobatics. With a BA (HONS) in Costume from the Arts University Bournemouth, her previous costume credits include *Touched* by Remix at the Southbank Centre, and *A Town Is Bourne* at the Shelley Theatre, Bournemouth.

## The Millers – Set, Lighting and Sound Design

The Millers are a clandestine group of individuals who work in the Grist To The Mill cellars and have produced designs for *The Autumn of Han, The Princess and The Pea, DiaoChan, The Empress and Me, An Evening With Miss Wong, The Unknown Soldier, Gratiano,* and *Monkey and The White Bone Demon*.

## Henry Fielding's
# Tom Jones

Adapted For the Stage by
## Ross Ericson

*For Michelle, because it makes her smile.*

## Characters

**Henry Fielding,** *the narrator and author of this work.*

**Tom Jones**, *the adopted son of Mr Allworthy, a typical young lad out to enjoy life.*

**Sophia**, *the young daughter of Squire Weston, schooled to be a lady but not always the shrinking violet.*

**Mr Allworthy**, *adopted father to Tom and Blifil and neighbour to Squire Weston, a wealthy man.*

**Mr Thwackam**, *Tom's tutor, whose chosen method is to beat the learning into them.*

**Blifil**, *Allworthy's nephew and the very opposite to young Tom.*

**Squire Weston**, *neighbour to Allworthy, father to Sophia, a country squire who loves all the country pursuits.*

**Mrs Weston**, *the Squire's sister. A lady of refinement who despairs at her brother's manners and is determined to ensure Sophia has a future whether she wants one or not.*

**Mrs Honour**, *maid servant to Sophia.*

**Northerton**, *an Ensign in the army. A drunk, a bully and possibly a coward.*

**Mrs Waters**, *a widow woman, and merry with it.*

**The Landlady**, *owner of the Inn At Upton.*

**Mrs Fitzpatrick**, *cousin to Sophia and a woman of fashion who is fleeing a husband who has turned out to be not what she thought.*

**Mr Fitzpatrick**, *her husband, a red-headed Irishman with a temper.*

**Lady Bellaston**, *a lady of refinement who passes the time by hunting young men in London society.*

**Lord Fellamar**, *a lord, with all the arrogance and stupidity that comes with the title.*

*Note: You are free to make your own choices, but we performed the play as if Henry Fielding had got some of his friends together to perform 'his play' at a country house gathering. Our set was a Georgian drawing room, which was augmented for the various scenes, and our cast doubled and trebled up in some cases, which can bring its own humour.*

# Act One

### Scene One – Allworthy's House

*A Georgian drawing room.* **Fielding** *enters as if pushed – it is his first time on stage.*

**Fielding**   It is said that we can liken theatre to a great meal. We, the hosts, humbly present to you several courses that we feel compliment each other both in taste and diversity in the vain hope that we cater for all palates at the table. But we are not gentlemen giving a private or eleemosynary treat. We are here for the ordinary public, and all persons are welcome for their money. If we were gentlemen entertainers, providing for those that perceive themselves to be of a higher intellect, we provide what we please but, with ordinary folk – men who pay for what they eat (*indicating the audience*) if anything is not agreeable to their taste, they will cause effect to boil the perpetrator with his own ham – and I do mean ham.

**N/O**   Get on with it.

**Fielding**   So to prevent giving offence to any customers by way of disappointment – and to save our bacon – we shall provide a bill of fare. Our provision then is none other than human nature. It shall be served up in that more plain and simple manner that is found in the country, but hashed and ragoud with all the high French and Italian seasoning of sex and vice – and all finished off with coffee and a mint. Ladies and gentlemen, please kindly take your seats for the 'History of Tom Jones'.

**Fielding** *moves to the side to allow* **Tom** *and* **Thwackam** *to enter. They are in a silent, heated conversation.*

**Fielding**   The hero of our tale – if he is that – is Mr Tom Jones. He is, unfortunately, a bastard, and I mean that in the truest sense of the term. The parson, Mr Thwackam, is Tom's tutor, and as usual, they are engaged in an ethical debate, an argument that I believe Mr Thwackam will conclude in his usual fashion.

*Exit* **Fielding**.

**Thwackam**    Okay, boy, jacket off, breeches down, assume the position.

**Tom** *drops his trousers reluctantly and bends over.* **Thwackam** *produces a cane.*

Now it is known full well that you shot that partridge upon Squire Weston's land.

**Tom**    As I have said; I did not shoot the bird on Squire Weston's land, it merely fell on it.

**Thwackam**    Oh that was clumsy of him, wasn't it?

*A stroke.*

**Tom**    But . . .

**Thwackam**    Silence, boy. You were caught red-handed by Squire Weston himself, and if you do not tell me who was with you you will not sit down for a week. (*Pause.*) You do not answer? (*Stroke.*) Speak, you obstinate child – who was with you? (*Stroke.*) I will have an answer if it kills you. (*Stroke.*) *Castigo te non quod habeam, sed quod amem – construe.*

**Tom**    I chastise thee not out of hatred, but out of love.

**Thwackam**    Good. (*Stroke.*) Look now, we know who was with you. It was Black George, wasn't it? Well, wasn't it? You only have to confirm our suspicions and we will forget all about this. Well? Answer me, damn you. (*Stroke.*) It was him, wasn't it?

**Allworthy** *enters unseen.*

**Tom**    I was alone.

**Thwackam**    Liar!

*Stroke.*

**Allworthy**    Enough, Mr Thwackam. Enough I say.

**Thwackam**    But, Mr Allworthy, I am yet to have an answer from the young reprobate – I am not yet satisfied.

**Allworthy**    But I am. You have carried this severity beyond what I had intended. I believe I have been mistaken. (*To* **Tom**.) I am convinced, my dear child, that my suspicions have wronged you.

**Tom**    Oh, sir . . .

**Thwackam**    He is lying.

**Allworthy**    If he is I believe you have chastised him enough for it.

**Tom** *pulls up his breeches.*

**Thwackam**    A further whipping will bring the truth to his lips.

**Allworthy**    Enough, I said. Now, leave us Tom, go and get yourself cleaned up.

**Tom**    Thank you sir.

**Tom** *exits.*

**Thwackam**    Spare the rod and spoil the child. If I were to have him for a few more moments I guarantee you, sir, we would know who his accomplice was.

**Allworthy**    This is the end to the matter, Mr Thwackam. If he is concealing the truth – if he is guilty – then he can have no other motive but a mistaken point of honour.

**Thwackam**    Honour, honour? Mere stubbornness and obstinacy – give me just ten more minutes and I will soon have it out of him.

**Allworthy**    Leave him be, Mr Thwackam – I sometimes feel you enjoy your work too much.

**Thwackam**    Very well, I can do no more. I wash my hands of him. He is not to be governed. It would have been better, sir, if you had left him in the gutter in which he was born.

**Allworthy**    I assured Jenny Jones that the boy would want for nothing.

**Thwackam**    A promise to a slut – you were far too lenient on her, Mr Allworthy.

**Allworthy**    It was enough I did to banish her from her family and friends, besides, my sister was only too happy to look after young Tom and bring him up as a companion to my nephew.

**Thwackam**    Hardly a fitting one for Mr Blifil. If only Tom was half as virtuous as he.

**Allworthy**    My nephew is a virtuous man indeed, but he worries me. He has a sullen countenance that I fear is wholly the fault of my sister.

**Thwackam**    I understand that his father, Captain Blifil, God rest his soul, was an ill-tempered man with a penchant for the wicked ways of the world.

**Allworthy**    I am afraid that was so. His death was due to drink. And God forgive me when I say my sister was better off without him.

**Thwackam**    She has never married again?

**Allworthy**    No, and I hold out little hope that that may change.

**Thwackam**    I was lead to believe she was a woman of some beauty.

**Allworthy**    My sister's only beauty is her large dowry.

**Thwackam**    Oh, large is it?

**Allworthy**    She has neglected young Blifil, though. I fear she sees too much of his father in him, and has spent so much time abroad I feel the poor boy would no longer recognise her. Aye, she is to blame for his dour demeanour.

**Thwackam**    A rich woman, though?

**Blifil** *bursts onto the stage holding his bloody nose, closely followed by* **Tom**.

**Blifil**    Uncle, Uncle, look at my dose – look! He hit my dose.

**Allworthy**    What has occurred?

**Blifil**    Tom hit me.

**Tom**    He called me a beggarly bastard.

**Allworthy**    Is that so?

**Blifil**    Such profane words have never passed my lips.

**Thwackam**    I can assure you, Mr Allworthy, that such a phrase is beyond Master Blifil's character.

**Tom**    He did so.

**Blifil**    I did not. It's no wonder, those who will tell one fib will hardly trouble to stick at another. If I had told my master such a wicked fib as you have done, I should be ashamed to show my face.

**Tom**    You little . . .

**Thwackam**    What fib?

**Blifil**    He told you that nobody was with him a-shooting when he killed the partridge; but he confessed it to me that Black George, the gamekeeper, was there. And he said – yes you did, deny it if you can – that he would not have confessed the truth though Mr Thwackam had cut him to pieces.

**Thwackam**    Oh, oh, so this is your mistaken notion of honour, Mr Allworthy.

**Allworthy**    Is this true, child?

**Tom**   Sir, I scorn a lie as much as anyone but my honour engaged me to act as I did. George had begged me not to trespass onto the gentleman's land but I ignored him. Indeed, sir, it could hardly be called a lie that I told, for the poor fellow was entirely blameless of the whole matter. He only followed me to prevent more mischief. Do, pray sir, forgive poor old George.

**Allworthy**   I shall think on it.

**Thwackam** (*Flexing the cane.*)   Meanwhile I think . . .

**Allworthy**   No, Mr Thwackam. Now be off with the pair of you.

**Blifil**   But Uncle . . .

**Thwackam**   Mr Allworthy . . .

**Allworthy**   Off with you, and live more peaceably together.

*Exit* **Tom** *and* **Blifil**.

**Thwackam**   I shall take the birch once more to that boy's backside.

**Allworthy**   You shall do no such thing, Mr Thwackam. His actions, after all, were honourable.

**Thwackam**   Honourable, my arse.

**Allworthy**   You forget yourself, Mr Thwackam.

**Thwackam**   To remit punishment of such crimes is to encourage them.

**Allworthy**   There was fortitude in Tom's actions.

**Thwackam**   Fortitude, fortitude? There may have been, but falsehood is adverse, and they do not agree or unite together. And in my opinion to confound virtue and vice requires an even greater castigation. Look at Master Blifil. He is the epitome of virtue. Bringing truth to light is the duty of every religious man.

**Allworthy**   Yes, but I sometimes wonder at his motives. Now you will not lay a finger on Tom for what has passed.

**Thwackam**   But . . .

**Allworthy**   Not one finger.

**Thwackam**   It is certain that the boy will be spoiled.

*Exit* **Thwackam**.

**Allworthy**   Black George, however, has basely suffered Tom to undergo heavy punishment for his sake, where he could have prevented it by making the discovery himself. He shall not go without punishment and shall be dismissed from my service.

*Blackout.*


**Scene Two – The Woods**

*The lights come up on a woodland scene.* **Molly** *is collecting mushrooms.* **Tom** *enters, rubbing his backside.*

**Tom**   That Thwackam enjoys his work too much.

**Molly**   Hello, Master Tom. What ails you?

**Tom**   Oh Molly, it is nothing. I was just on my way to see your father, I feel that my foolishness has cost him dear.

**Molly**   'Tis the poaching, ain't it? They knows he was with you. Oh, I knew it, I knew it.

**Tom**   I'm so sorry, Molly. I took a beating and never said a word, but Blifil found out and gave up George's name to Mr Allworthy.

**Molly**   Oh, he's such a fool, I told him . . . a beating?

**Tom**   Yes Molly.

**Molly**   Oh, you poor boy. Does it hurt?

**Tom**   Well . . .

**Molly**   Come on let's have a look.

**Tom**   No Molly . . .

**Molly**   It's the least I can do.

**Tom**   But Molly, you can't . . .

**Molly**   Don't be such a big baby.

*She spins* **Tom** *around and whips down his breeches.*

**Tom**   Molly!

**Molly**   Good Lord. We must get something on that. I have somewhere here (*she starts looking in the bag she is carrying*) an ointment of my mother's – it's for nettles so may take the sting out.

**Tom**   But I have to see your father.

**Molly**   You never mind him. He be big enough and ugly enough to look after himself. Ah, here it is.

*She bends him over again and starts applying the ointment to his rump.*

**Tom**   Molly!

**Molly**   How does that feel?

**Tom**   Well it's . . . Oooh, it's . . .

**Molly**   Is it doing the trick?

**Tom**   I should say so.

**Molly**   It may feel a little stiff for a while.

**Tom**   I'm sorry?

**Molly**   But you will soon feel some relief.

**Tom**   Will I?

**Molly** *turns him round to face her and starts to do up the buttons on his breeches.*

**Molly**   Oh yes, I think I do feel a little tightness.

**Tom**   Do you? And do you have something for that?

**Molly**   I might have.

**Tom**   Oh Molly.

**Molly**   Oh, Master Tom.

**Tom**   Oh Molly.

*She drags him off into the 'bushes' off stage. Just as* **Thwackam** *and* **Blifil** *enter.* **Blifil** *has seen the two figures darting into the bushes but* **Thwackam** *has not.*

**Thwackam**   . . . and if your fine mother is available to visitors, I would like to take the opportunity to meet with her, to discuss your education.

**Blifil**   Wanton Hussy!

**Thwackam**   Is she?

**Blifil**   Wanton hussy and a degenerate bastard.

**Thwackam**   I can assure you, sir, that my parents were married, and I think you should refrain from referring to your mother in such a . . .

**Blifil**   Mr Thwackam, over there, in the bushes, can you see?

**Thwackam**   What?

**Blifil**   I saw some wench and a fellow retire among them, which I doubt not is for some wicked purpose.

**Thwackam** (*Excitedly.*)   What? Really? Good Lord. (*Suddenly composing himself.*) Good Lord. You know it never ceases to amaze me what an unholy place this Somersetshire is. Somerset women are looser than a five-year-old's shoe laces. They spend so much time on their backs I am surprised they still have use of their legs. The blame sits at your uncle's feet, having mitigated that just and wholesome rigour of the law that allots a severe punishment to loose wenches.

**Blifil**   I fear you are right, Mr Thwackwam.

**Thwackam**   Then it is our duty, Master Blifil, to rectify this situation as best we can.

**Blifil**   Indeed, Mr Thwackam.

*They both peer off stage into the bushes.*

**Thwackam**   You sir, unhand that wench at once and come out here. Yes, you sir.

**Tom** *emerges from the bushes with his clothes in disarray.*

**Thwackam**   Fie upon it, Mr Jones, is it possible you could be the person?

**Tom**   Ah yes, you see, yes it is possible that I should be here, and as usual so are you.

**Thwackam**   And who is that wicked slut with you?

**Tom**   Ah, now if I have any wicked slut with me I shall not let you know who she is.

**Thwackam**   I command you to tell me immediately.

**Tom**   I shall not.

**Thwackam**   I am resolved to find out who she is.

**Tom**   And I am resolved that you shall not.

**Thwackam** *advances,* **Tom** *pushes him back.*

**Blifil**   Why you . . .

**Blifil** *lunges in and* **Tom** *punches him on the nose.*

**Blifil**   Oh doh, not again.

**Thwackam** *pushes past* **Tom** *who grabs him by the coat tails and swings him around. Pulling away they size each other up. After several swings* **Tom** *catches* **Thwackam** *in the stomach.* **Blifil** *gets up and is laid out by a head butt from* **Tom**. *Enter* **Sophia** *and* **Mrs Weston**.

**Mrs Weston**   Good Lord, child, avert your eyes.

*Just as* **Thwackam** *is about to rejoin the fight* **Mrs Weston** *starts laying into him with her parasol.*

**Mrs Weston**   Are you not ashamed to act in such a way in front of ladies? Barbarians, Philistines.

**Thwackam**   Madam, madam please . . . *pax.*

*She stops hitting him.*

**Mrs Weston**   Mr Thwackam I thought better of you. Look at you. (*At* **Blifil**.) Oh the poor lad. I have some smelling salts. (*She pulls the salts from her bag.*) You man, hold his head. (**Tom** *takes hold of* **Blifil**'s *head.*)

**Sophia**   Oh dear. Aunt, I do not feel . . .

**Sophia** *faints.* **Tom** *drops* **Blifil**'s *head and catches her.*

**Mrs Weston**   Oh, Sophia, my poor child. (*To the men.*) See what your antics have done.

*She administers the salts and* **Sophie** *comes round.*

**Sophia** (*Flirtatiously.*)   Oh, Mr Jones. (*Then notices her aunt.*) Oh, Auntie.

**Mrs Weston**   My dear girl, how do you feel?

**Sophia**   I think I am recovered.

**Tom** (*offering his arm*)   Miss Weston.

**Sophia**   Thank you, Mr Jones. (**Tom** *helps* **Sophia** *to her feet.*) Auntie, I wonder if Mr Jones would be kind enough to lend me his arm I think I should like to return to the house.

**Mrs Weston**   Of course, my dear. Mr Jones?

**Tom**   It would be a pleasure, madam.

**Tom** *and* **Sophia** *exit.*

**Mrs Weston**   Now, Mr Thwackam, what was the cause of this quarrel?

**Thwackam**    I believe the cause is not far off, madam. If you beat the bushes well you may find her.

**Mrs Weston**    Her? You have been fighting over a woman?

**Thwackam**    Madam I have been buffeted by a boy . . .

**Mrs Weston**    You've been what?

**Thwackam**    Buffeted . . . attacked. Attacked whilst endeavouring to do my duty in detecting and bringing to justice a wanton harlot.

**Mrs Weston**    I see, I see. I may have wronged you, Mr Thwackam. It is obvious to me that you and Mr Blifil here are men of great responsibility. Well, where is this girl? Show her to me.

**Blifil**    There madam, in those bushes.

**Blifil** *points off stage.*

**Mrs Weston**    Good Lord, so she is. She is practically naked!

**Blifil**    Yes, not a stitch on her.

**Thwackam**    Yes, amazing . . . (*They look at him.*) Amazing the depravity of it all.

**Mrs Weston**    I think I have seen enough.

**Thwackam** (*Aside.*)    I haven't.

**Thwackam** *starts to clandestinely wave and flirt with the unseen* **Molly**.

**Mrs Weston**    Mr Blifil, will you walk me back?

**Blifil**    I would be honoured, madam.

**Mrs Weston**    Mr Thwackam? Mr Thwackam?

**Thwackam**    Madam? Oh, I was thinking I should stay and . . . and, mmm, I should stay and educate this young strumpet about the error of her ways.

**Mrs Weston**    I think, sir, that it would be better if you returned with us, for I would be concerned about who was educating who. Come, sir.

**Thwackam** *follows* **Blifil** *and* **Mrs Weston** *off stage, only to return moments later and scurry off into the bushes after* **Molly**.

*Blackout.*


**Scene Three – Weston's Garden**

*The lights come up on a formal garden. There is a bench centre stage.* **Fielding** *enters.*

**Fielding**    Now Mrs Weston, the tyrant with the parasol, is the sister of Mr Allworthy's next door neighbour – Squire Weston. Yes, that's right, the same gentleman that caught Tom with the bird – the partridge that is – and (*he moves to one side to allow* **Sophia** *and* **Tom** *to enter*) Sophia is his daughter. Now, although you will see the personalities of Squire Weston and Mr Allworthy are complete opposites, the families have been associated for many years and Tom is favoured company in the Weston house, due to his sporting achievement in the field. Squire Weston's thoughts mainly being either in the field, the stable, the kennel or the tavern. Miss Sophia Weston is the only thing, it is rumoured, that the squire loves more than his horses, dogs and guns.

**Weston** (*Off stage.*)    I love my daughter more than any horse.

**Fielding**    She is a young lady of obvious charm and has caught the eye of many a suitor, including that of Mr Blifil, but she only has eyes for Tom. Now the fate of Black George and his family hang heavy on poor Tom's heart and he seizes this opportunity to solicit the help of young Sophia to gain favour with her father on behalf of Black George . . .

**Tom**    Madam, are you feeling better?

**Sophia**    Oh, much better thank you, Mr Jones.

**Tom**   I did not realise you had returned from Bath.

**Sophia**   I have been back but a few days.

**Tom**   I would have hardly have recognised you – you have grown so . . .

**Sophia** (*Blushing.*)   Oh, Mr Jones.

**Tom**   May I ask you something Miss Sophia?

**Sophia**   Well I . . .

**Tom**   Oh, I do apologise, if it is not convenient I could . . .

**Sophia**   No please Mr Jones, come sit with me.

**Tom**   Thank you. (*They sit on the garden bench.*) It is a favour I have to ask.

**Sophia**   Why, sir, I would oblige you in any way that I can, that is within the bounds that are available to a lady, so please, what is your request?

**Tom**   I am not sure how I should begin. It is such a favour that a man should ask of such a lady as you.

**Sophia** (*Intrigued.*)   Oh, really?

**Tom**   I am not sure of the right words, or indeed how to go about it.

**Sophia**   I am sure a gentleman, like yourself, has a greater understanding of these things than I.

**Tom**   Oh my dear Sophia, you are so understanding. But to ask such a thing.

**Sophia**   Oh, Mr Jones (*becoming a little excited*) you make me blush.

**Tom** (*Standing.*)   No, I cannot. It would be impudent of me.

**Sophia**   But you must.

**Tom**   No, I must not.

**Sophia** (*Standing.*)   Mr Jones I insist.

**Tom**   No, what I wish to ask should not pass from a gentleman to a lady.

**Sophia**   I'm sure it has before and will again. Please, I beseech you, ask me.

**Tom**   You will not be offended?

**Sophia**   I promise you I will not.

**Tom**   Well then, if you insist. I want you . . .

**Sophia**   Yes.

**Tom**   I want you to make pleadings on my behalf to your father . . .

**Sophia** (*Getting the wrong end of the stick.*)   Oh, Mr Jones.

**Tom**   For him to take Black George into his employment.

**Sophia**   Oh Mr . . . I'm sorry?

**Tom**   It is through my actions that he has lost his job and he and his large family now find themselves facing a hard future. He is one of the most honest men in the county and is well qualified for the position of gamekeeper.

**Sophia** (*Sightly put out.*)   Is this the great favour you ask me?

**Tom**   I am sorry. It is indeed unworthy of me to ask you such a thing. I will leave and never bother you again.

**Sophia**   NO! No, I shall make the petition to my father, though I cannot promise you much success; but I will not quit his presence without obtaining an answer.

**Tom**   Oh, Miss Weston, how can I ever thank you.

**Sophia** *gives the audience a knowing look as the lights fade to black.*


## Scene Four – The Hunt

*A hunting horn sounds. Appropriate hunting music rises up and the lights come up just as* **Fielding** *enters nervously at a run, wearing a fox's tail and ears.*

**Fielding** 'Tis the season of the fox, and Squire Weston never misses any opportunity of molesting any of God's creatures.

*He looks nervously about before running off, just before the hunters erupt onto the stage –* **Tom**, **Weston**, **Mrs Weston**, **Sophia** *and* **Blifil** *– all galloping on the spot on imaginary horses.*

**Weston** Come on you jolly dogs.

*All exit except for* **Sophia** *and* **Tom**. **Sophia**'s *'horse' stumbles and she is thrown off only to be caught by* **Tom**, *and they land on the floor together. The music stops.*

**Tom** My dear Sophia, are you harmed?

**Tom** *helps* **Sophia** *to her feet. He is favouring his left arm.*

**Sophia** I think I am safe Mr Jones (*noticing his arm*) I hope you have not come to any mischief.

**Tom** Be not concerned madam. Heaven be praised you have escaped so well, considering the danger you were in. If I have broke my arm, I consider it a trifle in comparison of what I feared upon your account.

**Sophia** Broke your arm, heaven forbid.

**Tom** I beg you will suffer me first to take care of you. I have a right hand yet at your service to help you into the next field, where we have but a very little walk to your father's house.

*Blackout.*

## Scene Five – Squire Weston's House

*The lights come up on* **Squire Weston**'s *house. It is a little unkempt – a certain lack of polish.* **Sophia** *is sat in a chair, lost in a book,* **Squire Weston** *is at the table cleaning a shotgun.* **Fielding** *enters.*

**Fielding** When they finally get back to the house of Squire Weston the rest of the hunting party had returned. The local doctor was called out for Master Tom; who examines him and announces that his arm was indeed broken. The arm is reset (**Tom** *screams off stage*) and Tom sent to rest for several days, leaving the Weston household to comtemplate Sophia's lucky escape.

**Mrs Weston** *enters*.

**Mrs Weston**    What are you doing brother?

**Weston**    I am contemplating Sophia's lucky escape.

**Fielding**    Now Mrs Weston has spent her life greatly improving her mind. She is well read in literature, history and politics, and fancies herself above the station of a country spinster, and like all women of a certain age she enjoys in dabbling with other people's love lives, having none of her own. This young Sophia is about to discover much to her dismay.

**Fielding** *exits*.

**Mrs Weston**    Pray, brother, have you not noticed something extraordinary in my niece lately?

**Weston**    No, not I, is there anything the matter with the girl?

**Mrs Weston**    I think there is, and something of much consequence too.

**Weston**    Why she doth not complain of anything, and she hath had the smallpox.

**Mrs Weston**    Brother, young girls are liable to other distempers besides the smallpox and sometimes possibly much worse.

**Weston**    I beg of you, if you know what ails my daughter, aquaint me with it immediately, you know I love her more than my best mare. I would send to the world's end for the best physician for her.

**Mrs Weston**   Nay, nay, the distemper is not so terrible. But I believe, and I promise you, I was never more deceived in my life, that my niece be not most desperately in love.

**Weston**   How? In love without acquainting me. I'll disinherit her. I'll turn her out of doors, stark naked, without a farthing. Is all my kindness, all my fondness over her come to this, to fall in love without asking me leave?

**Mrs Weston**   But you will not turn her out of doors before you know whether you shall approve her choice. Suppose she should have fixed on the very person that whom you yourself would wish. I hope you would not be angry then.

**Weston**   No, no, that would make a difference. If she marries the man I would have her then she may love who she pleases.

**Mrs Weston**   That spoken like a sensible man. I believe the person she hath chosen is the person you would choose for her.

**Weston**   Well who is the man?

**Mrs Weston**   What do you think of Mr Blifil?

**Weston**   Blifil?

**Mrs Weston**   I have noticed this since I came across him, Mr Thwackam and young Tom Jones the other day. She fainted away when she did see him lying breathless on the ground. And I know that this was the cause of her melancholy that night at supper; and the next morning, and indeed ever since.

**Weston**   I knew my little Sophy was a good girl and wouldn't fall in love to make me angry.

**Mrs Weston**   I thought you might see it that way, Mr Blifil is a fine young man.

**Weston**   Bugger Blifil, just think of the land. Nothing can lie as handy together as our two estates. Well sister, what do you advise me to do?

**Mrs Weston**   I think you may propose the match to Allworthy yourself.

**Weston**   Myself? Well I will propose it, but what if he should refuse me?

**Mrs Weston**   The match is too advantageous to be refused.

**Weston**   I don't know that. Allworthy is a queer bitch – money hath no effect on him.

**Mrs Weston**   Brother, do you think Mr Allworthy hath more contempt for money than other men because he professes more?

**Weston**   If you are sure, sister?

**Mrs Weston**   I am sure, brother.

**Weston**   Then I will write to him immediately, come sister, I will need your help with the letter.

**Weston** *and* **Mrs Weston** *exit and* **Tom** *enters with his arm in a sling.*

**Tom**   Miss Weston.

**Sophia**   Oh, Mr Jones, how are you? Please sit down – rest yourself.

*She places him in a chair and starts to fuss over him.*

**Tom**   Please Sophia, don't . . .

**Sophia**   Now Mr Jones I should be allowed to fuss over the man that saved my life. How is your arm? Would you like another cushion?

**Tom**   No, thank you, it is much better. Still a bit sore, but the doctor says I should have it out of the sling in a few days.

**Sophia**    I am glad to hear you are recovering well. I am sorry that I have caused you so much trouble.

**Tom**    My dear Miss Weston, it was not trouble at all. It was, indeed, an honour to be of service to you.

**Sophia**    You have been so kind to me, Mr Jones. Though I have felt that you have neglected me somewhat since my return from Bath. We spent many a day together when we were children but now you seem somewhat distant.

**Tom**    Oh, my dearest Sophia, I am sorry that you feel it is so, but you have returned from Bath a young lady and sometimes I feel it difficult to acquaint you with the girl I once knew. You have become so beautiful.

**Sophia**    Oh, Mr Jones, you make me blush. Are these the words you use on the girls from the village?

**Tom**    My darling Sophie, please do not think of me that way. I am afraid my reputation is somewhat out of hand. You should not believe all that you hear.

**Sophia**    And what do I hear, Mr Jones?

**Tom**    I should hate to hazard a guess, madam. Somerset entertains some of the best tall-story tellers in the kingdom. But the truth is, my dearest Sophie, that I now only have eyes for one.

**Sophia**    Do I know her?

**Tom**    Better than I.

**Sophia**    And you profess that your heart is set on her?

**Tom**    I do. And you, Sophia, have you a beau?

**Sophia**    There is one who I believe has set my heart on fire.

**Tom**    He is a truly lucky man. I hope he appreciates his good fortune.

**Sophia**    I believe he does not even know of my affection for him.

**Tom**    Then he must be a fool.

**Sophia**    And your amour, Mr Jones? Does she recognise your intentions?

**Tom**    Oh, I only wish that she did. But I am too much the coward to make my intentions known.

**Sophia**    Then you should, Mr Jones.

**Tom**    But if she spurns my advances I should be desolate, and I fear I may lose her company permanently.

**Sophia**    Perhaps I may repay the favour you have done me. If you acquaint me with her name then I may approach her for you.

**Tom**    Oh Sophie, you put me in such a position.

**Sophia**    I do not understand, Mr Jones. I assure you I will be most discreet. I hope you feel you can confide in me.

**Tom**    It is not that I cannot confide in you. Oh Sophie, can't you see? It is you I have been talking about.

**Sophia**    Oh Tom, this is so unexpected.

**Tom**    I know, I should not have told you.

**Sophia**    No, Mr Jones . . .

**Tom**    I shall not hold it against you if you wish not to see me again.

**Sophia**    But . . .

**Tom**    I can only wish you and your true love happiness.

**Sophia**    My true love?

**Tom**    Yes, your true love. The man you were talking about.

**Sophia**    But that was you Tom.

**Tom**    I'm sorry?

**Sophia**    I was referring to you, my darling Tom.

**Tom**    Me? Oh Sophie.

**Sophia**    Oh Tom.

*They go to embrace but are interrupted as* **Mrs Honour** *enters and passes directly between them.*

**Mrs Honour**    Afternoon ma'am, Mr Jones.

**Mrs Honour** *starts dusting purposefully and the lovers realise they have missed their chance.*

**Tom**    I shall beg your leave, Miss Weston. I have some affairs I need to take care of.

**Sophia**    Of course Mr Jones.

**Tom**    Mrs Honour.

**Tom** *exits.*

**Mrs Honour**    La ma'am, Mr Jones is so pretty a gentleman and so courageous. He must have been in terrible pain. I know men who would have cursed the surgeon for doing that to his arm – but not Mr Jones. What a marvellous handsome man. How beauteous his person. It is so perfect in his form, so exquisite in its muscularity, and his skin ma'am, how beautifully white it is.

**Sophia**    Mrs Honour, you are certainly in love with this young fellow.

**Mrs Honour**    I in love, ma'am? Upon my word I assure you, ma'am. Upon my soul, ma'am, I am not.

**Sophia**    Why if you were I see no reason that you should be ashamed of it, for he is certainly a pretty fellow.

**Mrs Honour**    Yes, ma'am, that he is, the most handsomest man I ever saw in my life. Yes, as your la'ship say I don't know why I should be ashamed of loving him, though he is my betters. But to be sure, though Squire Allworthy hath made Mr Jones a gentleman, he was not so good as myself by birth. Nobody can say that I am base born.

**Sophia**   I wonder at your assurance at daring to talk thus of my father's friends. As regards to Mr Jones' birth, those who can say nothing more to his disadvantage may as well be silent – as I desire you will be for the future.

**Mrs Honour**   I am sorry I have offended your la'ship. Indeed I can call all the servants in the house to witness that whenever any talk has been about bastards I have always taken his part. I could tell your la'ship something, but I am afraid that it would offend you.

**Sophia**   What could you tell me Honour?

**Mrs Honour**   Nay, ma'am, to be sure, he mean't nothing by it, and so I would not have your la'ship offended.

**Sophia**   Prithee, tell me, I will know this instant.

**Mrs Honour**   Why ma'am, he came into the room one day when I was at work and there lay your la'ship's muff on the chair. And, to be sure, he puts his hand into it. 'La,' says I, 'Mr Jones you have stretched my lady's muff and spoiled it.' But he still kept his hands in it, and then he kissed it. To be sure, I hardly ever saw such a kiss in my life that he gave it.

**Sophia**   My muff? He did know it was mine?

**Mrs Honour**   He did. He kissed it again and again, and said it was the prettiest muff in the world. 'La, sir', says I, 'you have seen it a hundred times.' 'Yes, Mrs Honour,' says he, 'but I never notice her ladship's muff when she is in the room.'

**Sophia**   As you say he meant nothing.

**Mrs Honour**   I hope your la'ship will not mention a word, for he gave me a crown never to mention it.

**Sophia**   Honour, you will not mention this anymore to me or to anybody else. It is clear that Mr Jones meant nothing by it.

**Mrs Honour**  Nay, madam, I protest he meant nothing. 'Yes,' says he, 'Honour, I . . .' oh, pardon your la'ship.

**Sophia**  Go on, you may mention anything you have not told me before.

**Mrs Honour**  If you wish, ma'am. 'Yes, Honour,' says he, 'I am not such a villain as to think of her in any other delight but as my goddess, as such I will always worship and adore her while I have breath.' This was all madam, to the best of my rememberence.

**Sophia**  Oh, Honour, I cannot abide . . .

**Mrs Honour**  Nay, ma'am, I was in a passion with him myself.

**Sophia**  Not a word to anyone.

**Mrs Honour**  I would rather cut out my tongue.

*Blackout.*


### Scene Six – Molly's Hovel

*Inside the tumbledown interior of a country cottage.* **Fielding** *enters.*

**Fielding**  So our lovers have found each other. But as Tom said, he has some affairs to deal with, for there are a few loose wom . . . ends that need to be tied up before Tom can pursue the lovely Sophia in earnest. One of those loose ends is Molly. So when his arm is well enough recovered that he could walk easily, without it slung in a sash, he stole forth to visit her.

**Tom** *enters and* **Fielding** *exits.*

**Tom**  Molly, Molly.

**Molly** *emerges half-dressed from behind a curtain, she makes sure the curtain is pulled across behind her. She seems a little nervous.*

**Molly**   Oh, Master Tom, I was not expecting you.

**Tom**   I can see that. Oh, how marvellous and beautiful you look.

**Molly**   Oh, Master Tom.

**Tom**   Seeing you like this makes me forget my purpose.

**Molly**   I haven't seen you for some time – I thought you had deserted me. Let me get myself decent and we can talk.

**Tom**   No, Molly, I have come to say goodbye.

**Molly**   Goodbye?

**Tom**   Yes, we can no longer carry on the way we have. Mr Allworthy has forbade me to see you, and I do not wish to bring ruin on us both. Now your father has achieved a position with Squire Weston you and your family should be safe. I have brought you a small token as a farewell present.

**Tom** *hands her a purse.*

**Molly** (*Bursting into tears.*)   And this is your love for me? To forsake me in this manner now that you have ruined me? How often, when I told you that all men are liars and grow tired of us as soon as ever they have had their wicked ways, how often have you sworn you would never foresake me? And now you turn out to be the same as them. What signifies the riches in the world to me without you (*she throws the purse at him*), now you have gained my heart, so you have, so you have.

**Tom**   But Molly you will soon find another man.

**Molly**   How can you mention another man to me? I can never love another man as long as I live. All other men are nothing to me. If the greatest squire in all the country would come a-suiting me tomorrow, I would not give my company to him. No, I shall always hate and despise the whole sex for your sake . . .

*The curtain suddenly falls down exposing a naked* **Thwackam**, *hiding his embarrassment with a tricorn hat.*

**Molly**   Oh, I am undone.

**Molly** *hastily exits.* **Tom** *laughs heartily.*

**Thwackam**   Well, sir, I see you enjoy this mighty discovery and, I dare say, take great delights in your thoughts of exposing me.

**Tom**   I think you have done that yourself. So that's why they call it a cocked hat!

**Thwackam**   If you consider the matter fairly, you will find that you are yourself only to blame.

**Tom**   I am to blame?

**Thwackam**   I am not guilty of corrupting innocence. I have done nothing for which the world will condemn me.

**Tom**   No need for explanations, I will not tell a soul. Unless you have a mind to discover it yourself this affair may remain a profound secret for me.

**Thwackam**   I promise you I will not betray myself. Things may be fitting to be done, but not fitting to be boasted of. For by the perverse judgement of the world, what often becomes the subject of censure is not only innocent but laudable.

**Tom**   Right, what can be more innocent than the indulgence of natural appetite, what can be more laudable than the propagation of our species.

**Thwackam**   To be serious with you, I profess they always appeared so to me.

**Tom**   You were of a different opinion when you first tried to uncover my affair with this girl.

**Thwackam**   I was merely condemning the corruption of innocence, a crime that I have already pointed out that I am not guilty of.

**Tom**   Be that as it may, it shall be your own fault, as I have promised, if you hear any more of this adventure. Behave kindly to the girl and I shall never open my lips concerning the matter to anyone. And Molly (*directed off stage*) do be faithful to your friend.

*Offstage* **Molly** *lets out a wail.* **Tom** *exits.*

**Thwackam**   Arrogant little bastard. I can no more trust you, Mr Jones, that I would a bishop in a brothel. I must ensure your downfall to keep the sanctity of my good name. Only by besmirching you can I ensure that anything that you say about me can be construed as nothing but lies. Oh, you have made me an even more consistent enemy than before. Vengeance is mine, saith the Lord. Dear Lord – wreak it.

*Blackout.*

### Scene Seven – Squire Weston's House

*Lights up on* **Sophia** *sat playing the harpsichord badly,* **Tom** *is stood by her – the air is electric.* **Fielding** *enters.*

**Fielding**   Summer ended, autumn passed, and then there came a harsh winter, but Tom and Sophia were kept warm by their love. Soon it was spring again and it wasn't only the sheep that were lambing.

**Fielding** *exits as* **Weston** *enters.*

**Weston**   Ah, Tom my lad, you here again?

**Weston** *waves an empty glass at him.* **Tom** *picks up from on top of the harpsichord and refills it.*

**Tom**   I find Miss Weston's playing exquisite.

**Weston** (*Removing cotton wool from an ear.*)   You what?

**Tom**   I said I find Miss Weston's playing exquisite.

**Weston**   Oh, you do? Right, yes, of course. (*Listens for a moment. She finishes the piece. They both clap politely.*) 'Ere I have just heard some news from the village. This morning a wench was brought forward before Mr Allworthy on the eve of bringing forth a bastard!

**Sophia**   And is this all your news, Father? I thought it might have been some public matter concerning the nation.

**Weston**   Well it only turns out to be Molly Seagrams, the daughter of Black George.

**Sophia**   Molly Seagrams?

**Weston**   Aye, 'er. Allworthy demanded of her who the father was but she refused to tell 'im. 'Ere, come along lad, drink up, the bottle is with you.

**Tom**   I have just remembered some urgent business I must attend to.

**Weston**   At this time of day?

**Tom**   May I beg your leave, sir?

*He gives* **Weston** *the bottle.*

**Weston**   Won't you stay for another bottle?

**Tom**   It is most urgent. Sir, Miss Weston.

**Tom** *exits.*

**Weston**   I don't know what the youth of today are coming to. What's got into the lad? Here we are 'aving a nice little chat 'bout black George's daughter then all of a sudden he's got to go shooting off. 'Ang on a minute. I smoke it, I smoke it; it's Tom . . .

**Sophia**   What is, Father?

**Weston**   Tom is the father of this bastard. Zooks, girl, you know that he recommended the father of her to me. Damn 'un. What sly bitch 'tis. Aye, aye, as sure as tuppence, Tom is the father o'that bastard.

**Sophia**   I should be very sorry for that.

**Weston**   Why sorry girl? Where's the mighty matter o'it? What man hath not got a bastard? Pox, it be more through luck than judgement. I warrant thee, we all have, and many a good time and often.

**Sophia**   Father you are pleased to be jocular, but I fear this may injure him with Mr Allworthy. And truly I must say he hath the character of being a little wild, but I see no harm in the young man or have heard of any. I must say that the young gentleman appears to me to be a very modest, civil man, and I should be sorry that he should do himself some injury with Squire Allworthy's opinion.

**Weston**   Pooh, injury with Allworthy? Why Allworthy loves a wench himself. Doth not all the country know whose son Tom is? No, no, he'll do no harm with her assure yourself; nor with anybody else. You have not the worst opinion of the young fellow for getting a bastard, have you girl? No, no, women like 'un the better for it.

**Mrs Weston** *enters.*

**Mrs Weston**   Ah brother, what pearls of swinish wisdom are you now forcing upon your poor daughter?

**Weston**   I was acquainting her with the ways of men.

**Mrs Weston**   Let's hope you have not spoiled her. I would hate for Sophia to wish to take holy orders when you have charged me to inform her of our news.

**Sophia**   What news, Father?

**Weston**   I shall leave your aunt to tell you my dear, I have urgent need of another bottle.

**Weston** *exits.*

**Sophia**   What is this news dear aunt?

**Mrs Weston**   I have news which will delight your very soul. Make me your confidant and I'll undertake that you shall be happy to the very extent of your wishes.

**Sophia**    La madam, I know not what you say. What, madam, should you suspect?

**Mrs Weston**    Consider you are talking to a friend, consider you are only revealing to me what I know already – a passion of which I highly approve.

**Sophia**    La madam, you come upon one so unawares. Is it possible you and my father can see with my eyes?

**Mrs Weston**    I tell you we do entirely approve. He is a charming young fellow.

**Sophia**    I know no other with such perfections. So brave and yet so gentle, so witty yet so inoffensive, so humane, so genteel, so handsome. What signifies his being base born with qualifications such as these?

**Mrs Weston**    Base born?

**Sophia**    Base born.

**Mrs Weston**    Mr Blifil base born?

**Sophia**    Blifil?

**Mrs Weston**    Aye, Mr Blifil. Mr Blifil – who else have we been talking of?

**Sophia**    Good heavens of Mr Jones, I thought. I am sure I know no other that deserves . . .

**Mrs Weston**    Tom Jones? Is it possible that you can think of allying yourself to a bastard?

**Sophia**    But Aunt . . .

**Mrs Weston**    Tom Jones! I would rather follow you to your grave than see you disgrace yourself and your family by such a match. You are the first, Miss Weston, aye the first of your name who ever entertained such a grovelling thought. A family so noted for the prudence of its women . . .

**Sophia**    Please, dear Aunt, I beg of you please do not reveal to my father what today you have drawn from me.

**Mrs Weston**    Why should I not, he has a right to know.

**Sophia**    I fear the violence of my father's temper. I have no inclination to offend him in any way.

**Mrs Weston**    Very well, only on one consideration shall I keep this secret from my brother.

**Sophia**    Yes Aunt?

**Mrs Weston**    That is that you will promise to entertain Mr Blifil this afternoon as your lover.

**Sophia**    But Aunt . . .

**Mrs Weston**    No buts – that is the condition.

**Sophia**    I cannot . . .

**Mrs Weston**    You have but one choice – take it or leave it.

**Mrs Weston** *exits leaving* **Sophia** *in tears. Lights down on stage.* **Blifil** *and* **Thwackam** *aside in a single spot.*

**Blifil**    I need your counsel Mr Thwackam.

**Thwackam**    If I can be of any assistance, it would be my pleasure.

**Blifil**    A messenger has arrived from my mother.

**Thwackam**    Indeed, how is she?

**Blifil**    She is dead.

**Thwackam**    Not well then. I am sorry to hear this, you have my condolences.

**Blifil**    I knew her not.

**Thwackam**    Indeed.

**Blifil**    The letter was not even addressed to me but my uncle.

**Thwackam**    Then should you not give it to Mr Allworthy?

**Blifil** *hands the letter to* **Thwackam**.

**Blifil**   I think not.

**Thwackam** (*Reading the letter.*)   Oh yes, I see.

**Blifil**   What should I do?

**Thwackam**   I think this letter has to be lost.

**Blifil**   But it says that . . .

**Thwackam**   I know what it says, and that is why you should lose it. Leave it to me. It will be my pleasure to ensure a swift resolution to your problem.

**Blifil**   How?

**Thwackam**   By removing the cause.

**Blifil**   If you do sir your loyalty shall be rewarded.

**Thwackam**   Thank you. (**Blifil** *exits*.) At last, a chance for revenge.

*The spot fades and lights come up on* **Sophia**. **Weston** *enters*.

**Weston**   Come, come, none of your maidenish airs I know all, I assure sister hath told me all.

**Sophia**   Is it possible that my aunt can have betrayed me already?

**Weston**   Aye, aye, betrayed you. Why you betrayed yourself. You showed your fancy very plainly. Oh, there, there, you cry because I'm going to marry you to the man that you are in love with. Your mother, I remember, whimpered and whined in just the same manner, but it was all over in two or three minutes after we were married. Mr Blifil is a brisk young man and will soon put an end to your squeamishness. Come, cheer up, cheer up, I expect him any minute.

**Sophia**   Oh no.

**Weston**   I knew you'd be happy.

**Blifil** *enters*.

**Blifil**  Squire Weston.

**Weston**  Ah, Mr Blifil, are ye ready for the hunt, sir?

**Blifil**  The hunt? Oh yes, sir, yes indeed I am.

**Weston**  Well follow her boy, follow her, and run her in. Never be bashful. Allworthy and I can finish all the matters between us tomorrow and we can have the wedding by the end of the week.

**Blifil**  There is nothing, sir, in this word which I so eagerly desire as an alliance with your family, except my union with the most amiable and deserving Sophia. You can easily imagine how impatient I must be to see myself in possession of my two highest wishes. But I fear offending the lady by endeavouring to hurry such a blessed event faster than with strict compliance to all the rules of decency and decorum will permit. But if by your interest, sir, she might be induced to dispense with any formalities . . .

**Weston**  Formalities! With a pox. All stuff and nonsense. I shall tell thee she shalt have thee. You will know the world better hereafter when you come to my age. Women never give their consent, man, if they can help it – 'tis not the fashion. If I'd stayed for her mother's consent I might have been a bachelor to this day. I tell thee thou shalt have her. Well go to her, my boy. Tight on the reigns, firm in the saddle, and don't spare the whip.

**Blifil**  Whip? (**Weston** *exits,* **Blifil** *sidles over to* **Sophia**.) Miss Weston.

**Sophia**  Mr Blifil.

**Blifil**  Miss Weston.

**Sophia**  Mr Blifil.

**Blifil**  I would just like to say . . .

**Sophia**  Yes?

**Blifil** I would just like to say I . . . (*noticing her breasts*) what a magnificent . . . I mean what perfect . . . What a lovely . . .

**Sophia** Dress?

**Blifil** Yes, dress. It is a most . . . It is a most pretty . . .

**Sophia** Colour?

**Blifil** Yes, colour.

*He sits next to her.*

**Blifil** The weather is rather . . .

**Sophia** Warm?

**Blifil** Yes, I am actually. I'm just trying to say how enamoured I am of your . . . your . . .

**Sophia** Eyes?

**Blifil** No br . . . Yes, yes eyes. That's it, your eyes, they are such a magnificent blue.

**Sophia** But they are green, Mr Blifil.

**Blifil** They are? Oh yes, your eyes, indeed, beautiful green eyes. And your . . .

**Sophia** Yes?

**Blifil** And your . . .

**Sophia** Yes?

**Blifil** Oh, my God, Sophia . . .

*He leaps on her. There is a struggle and she throws him off and stands up.*

**Sophia** Mr Blifil I've never been so . . .

**Blifil** . . . close? No, neither have I. (*Standing and straightening himself.*) Well madam, I shall withdraw now and, with your permission, call on you again tomorrow. (**Sophia** *bursts into tears.* **Blifil** *aside.*) Oh, what a magnificent catch. She is as beautiful in life as in fantasy. To obtain her hand has one great advantage – the rest of her comes with it.

**Weston** *enters.*

**Weston**   Well, my boy, how did you fare in the hunt?

**Blifil**   I think, if I might coin a hunting term, I've brought the prey to ground.

**Weston**   Well done you saucy dog.

**Blifil**   Thank you, sir, and I would like to express my enthusiasm for this process to be pushed forward at the greatest of speed.

**Weston**   And that it will be, Master Blifil.

**Blifil**   Now if I may take my leave, I wish to retire and prepare myself.

**Weston**   And what yerself?

**Blifil**   Prepare myself for the next interlude.

**Weston**   Now you won't be doing none of that until after the wedding. I shall see you in the morrow, sir. (**Blifil** *exits.*) Oh, my darling Sophy you have made me so pleased. You may choose what dresses and jewels you please. I do declare I have no other use for my fortune than to make you 'appy. Oh, my dearest, darling Sophy, you are my greatest love; I do love you more than anything in the world, you are my only joy on earth.

**Sophia**   My darling father, I do thank you for your kindness. And is it possible my papa can be so good as to place all his joy in his Sophy's happiness.

**Weston**   By the gods, your 'appiness is my only concern.

**Sophia** *takes hold of his hand and falls to the ground begging him.*

**Sophia**   My dear papa, please do not make me the most miserable creature on earth by forcing me to marry a man whom I detest.

**Weston**   What?

**Sophia**   This I entreat you sir, for your sake as well as my own, since you are so very kind to tell me your happiness depends on mine.

**Weston**   What?

**Sophia**   Oh, sir, not only does your poor Sophy's happiness but her very life, her being depends on you granting her request. I cannot marry Mr Blifil.

**Weston**   What?

**Sophia**   To force me into this marriage would be killing me.

**Weston**   You cannot marry Blifil?

**Sophia**   No, upon my soul I can't.

**Weston**   Then die and be damned.

**Sophia**   Oh, sir, take pity on me, I beseech you. Can you be unmoved while you see your Sophy in this dreadful condition? Would the best of fathers break my heart? Will he kill me by the most painful, cruel, lingering, death?

**Weston**   Rubbish, all stuff and nonsense, all maidenish tricks. Kill you indeed! Will marriage kill you?

**Sophia**   Oh, such a marriage is worse than death. I hate him, I detest him.

**Weston**   Detest him? You shall ha' 'un – you shall ha' 'un. I am resolved upon the match. And if you do not consent to this I shall throw you out onto the street without a farthing. (*He goes to exit and bumps into* **Tom**.) Oh, my dear boy whatever shall I do?

**Tom**   What is the matter, sir?

**Weston**   If only you knew, Tom.

**Tom**   Tell me, sir, maybe I can help?

**Weston**   My daughter, sir, is a disobedient bitch. An ingrate. How can she dishonour her father?

**Tom**   What can it be that your daughter has done to upset you?

**Weston**   Oh, woe is a man who has a daughter.

**Tom**   Sir, if I may have some time with your daughter maybe I can persuade her to obey you?

**Weston**   Would you do that for me Tom? Oh, what a good lad you are. Go to her see if you can make her see sense.

**Tom**   What is that matter concerning?

**Weston**   Marriage.

**Tom**   Marriage?

**Weston**   Aye, Allworthy and I have agreed that she should marry Mr Blifil.

**Tom**   Blifil?

**Weston**   Aye, Blifil. You can see what an advantage it would be for both or families. I am set on it. She will marry Blifil, or I will kick her out without a penny. Go to her boy, do your best.

*Exit* **Weston**.

**Tom**   Blifil? (*He goes to* **Sophia**.) Oh, my Sophia, what means this dreadful sight?

**Sophia**   Oh, Mister Jones, how came you here? Leave me, I beseech you.

**Tom**   Do not impose such a harsh command upon me – my heart bleeds faster than those tears flow.

**Sophia**   Oh, Mister Jones, why did you save my life? My death would have been the happier for both of us.

**Tom**   Happier for us both?

**Sophia**   Oh, Mister Jones, you know not what has passed this cruel afternoon.

**Tom**   I know all, my Sophia, your father has told me all and he himself has sent me here.

**Sophia**   My father has sent you?

**Tom**   Aye, to advocate for my odious rival, to solicit you in his favour.

**Sophia**   What would Mister Jones have me say?

**Tom**   Promise that you will never give yourself to Blifil.

**Sophia**   Be assured, I will never give him what is in my power to withhold.

**Tom**   Oh, Sophia, be so perfectly kind and go a little farther so that I may hope.

**Sophia**   What hope can I bestow? You know my father's intentions.

**Tom**   But I know your compliance with them cannot be compelled.

**Sophia**   I cannot – I cannot bear the thought of my father's misery.

**Tom**   He himself is the cause, by exacting power over you which nature hath not given him. Think on the misery I should suffer if I should lose you.

**Sophia**   Oh, Tom, you should fly from me to avoid your own destruction.

**Tom**   I fear no destruction, only the loss of my darling Sophia.

*Enter* **Weston** *and* **Mrs Weston** *aside.*

**Weston**   Oh, sister, sister, all is undone.

**Mrs Weston**   What ails you brother?

**Weston**   We shall be disgraced.

**Mrs Weston**   Pray tell, brother, what is it?

**Weston**   We shall be the laughing stock of the entire shire, nay the country.

**Mrs Weston**    Brother, stop your prattling and tell me what the matter is?

**Weston**    She has refused to marry Blifil.

**Mrs Weston**    Tell me it is not so.

**Weston**    'Tis so, the disobedient bitch. To marry him would kill her.

**Mrs Weston**    That is because your daughter is in love with your neighbour's bastard.

**Weston**    'Would the best of fathers break my heart?'

**Mrs Weston**    Did you hear me, brother? Your daughter is in love with a bastard.

**Weston**    What? Blifil?

**Mrs Weston**    No brother, have you heard a word I have said?

**Weston**    I cannot be listening to you when I have problems of my own.

**Mrs Weston**    Your daughter is enamoured of a bastard.

**Weston**    Blifil a bastard?

**Mrs Weston**    No, you fool, Sophia is enamoured of that rogue Tom Jones.

**Weston**    Jones, why the – I'll kick his arse, I'll send him a flick, I'll – oh, bugger.

**Mrs Weston**    What is it brother?

**Weston**    I have just sent him to Sophia's chamber.

**Mrs Weston**    Brother I know you are a fool but sometimes your stupidity surprises even me.

**Weston**    Odzooks, Jones, I'll lend him a flick, I'll kick his arse. (*He turns to* **Sophia** *and* **Tom**.) I shall kick your arse from here to Dorchester. Let me get hold of you, you bastard.

*As* **Weston** *chases* **Tom** *around the room* **Mrs Weston** *pulls* **Sophia** *to her feet.*

**Mrs Weston**   Come child.

**Sophia**   But Aunt . . . Tom!

**Mrs Weston** *drags* **Sophia** *off.*

**Weston**   I shall 'ave satisfaction of thee. So doth thy clothes and I will lick thee as well as wast ever licked in thy life. I shall kick your arse and you can kiss mine.

**Tom**   Sir, you will not provoke me with your abuse. I will not lift a hand against the father of the woman I love.

**Weston**   The woman you love? You impudent young rascal – stand still will ye.

**Allworthy** *enters and stands in front of* **Tom** *to protect him.*

**Allworthy**   Squire Weston, what the devil is the matter?

**Weston**   You have brought your bastard up to fine purpose, Allworthy.

**Allworthy**   What has he done?

**Weston**   My daughter hath fallen in love with him. I always thought no good would come o' breeding up a bastard like a gentleman and lettin' him come around folks' houses. If you let me get at him I'll spoil his caterwauling, I'll teach the son of a whore to meddle with meat for his master.

**Allworthy**   Squire Weston I am heartily sorry . . .

**Weston**   A pox on your sorrow. I have lost my only child; she was the joy of my heart, the only comfort in my old age. The son of a bitch was always good at finding a hare sitting. Little did I think when I loved him as a sportsman that he was poaching after my daughter.

**Allworthy**   What would you have me do on this occasion?

**Weston**    Keep the rascal away from my house. As for the girl I shall lock her up under guard. She shall marry Blifil, I am resolved to it, I shall have no other son-in-law.

*Exit* **Weston**.

**Allworthy**    You have left me little choice, Tom. I dealt lightly with Molly Seagram at your bequest and only now it reaches my ears that you may be the father of her child. (**Tom** *tries to speak*.) No, no excuses. She is no innocent and many have strayed in her direction and I could have forgiven you for this, but for your interference between Sophia and young Blifil, that is unforgivable. What were you thinking of? You have gone against my wishes and those of Squire Weston, and have tried to upset the future happiness of Sophia and my nephew. That is not an act of a gentleman. This is the last straw. I dearly love you, Tom, but I can no longer find it in my heart to forgive you. It pains me to say it but you must leave this house immediately. Go pack your things, I will provide you funds to start you off, but I never wish to see you again.

**Tom** *and* **Allworthy** *exit and* **Weston** *enters, getting ready for a day's riding.* **Mrs Weston** *enters almost immediately behind him.*

**Mrs Weston**    Your daughter is not to be found.

**Weston**    Not to be found? Zounds and damnation, blood and fury! Where, when, how, what – not to be found? Where is she not to be found?

**Mrs Weston**    La brother, you are always throwing yourself into such violent passions. If your daughter has left you then I am sorry for it, but it is all your own doings and you have nobody to thank but yourself. Had I been trusted entirely with the care of her education no such accident as this had ever befallen you. So that you must comfort yourself by thinking it was all your own doing and, indeed, what else can be expected from such an indulgence?

**Weston**   Zounds, sister, you are enough to make one mad. Have I indulged her? Have I given her her will? I told her if she disobeyed me I'd confine her to her chamber upon bread and water as long as she lived. You would provoke the patience of Job.

**Mrs Weston**   And you would provoke the patience of fifty Jobs.

**Weston**   Then take yer leave woman.

**Mrs Weston**   I shall, and no longer will I keep your council. You are on your own brother, adieu.

**Mrs Weston** *exits*.

**Weston**   Good bloody riddance. Hell and damnation, I'fackin bitch. I'll run her to ground, I'll catch up with her. (*To off stage.*) Fetch me my horse. (**Fielding** *enters*.) Do you have daughters, sir?

**Fielding**   No, sir, I am a happy bachelor.

**Weston**   Well I suggest ye stay that way. To marry one will make thee unhappy enough let alone siring one. They are more expensive, more disobedient, and more contrary than any hound – and if they were a horse you'd shoot them. Are you a drinking man, sir?

**Fielding**   I enjoy the odd glass, sir.

**Weston**   Then come, man, you may buy me a drink while we wait for the horses to be ready.

**Weston** *exits*.

**Fielding**   Well, we seem to be off to the bar, I suggest that you, yourselves, partake of refreshment before we carry on with our journey through the . . .

**Weston** (*Offstage.*)   Will you come on, sir, before the mob gets here.

**Fielding**   Coming Squire Weston.

*Curtain.*

## Act Two

### Scene One – The Inn At Upton

*There are two internal doors as well as the front door, stage left, and the back door, stage right. On stage there are several chairs and tables and a serving trestle.*

**Mrs Fitzpatrick** *sits at a table stage left, reading. At a table stage right is* **Ensign Northerton** *and* **Mrs Waters**. **Northerton** *is drunk and amorous.* **Fielding** *enters.*

**Fielding**   This is the famous inn at Upton . . .

**Northerton**   Bring me more ale.

**Fielding**   . . . halfway between Bridgewater and London.

*The* **Landlady** *appears from behind the trestle and brings a jug to* **Northerton**.

**Fielding**   Here we are expecting the imminent arrival of Tom Jones who, despite his initial intentions, will be arriving here shortly. You see, after leaving Mr Allworthy's house, he intended to head to Bristol, take on board a ship, and seek his fortune at sea. (*Takes a seat.*) Unfortunately, as is the humour of some country folk with strangers, he was given directions that have sent him entirely in the opposite direction. (**Northerton** *whispers something in* **Mrs Waters'** *ear. She slaps him and exits to her room behind one of the internal doors.* **Tom** *enters.*) Ah, speak of the devil.

**Tom** (*To* **Landlady**.)   Excuse me, madam, I am looking for a room for the night.

**Landlady**   No rooms left, it'll have to be a blanket on the floor.

**Tom**   Oh, I see . . .

**Landlady**   Would you care for a drink and a bite to eat?

**Tom**    Yes, yes, that would be grand, it has been a long and tiring day.

**Northerton**    Please, sir, join me if you will.

**Tom**    Why, that is most kind of you, sir.

**Northerton** *fills a mug for* **Tom**.

**Northerton**    Will you toast the king with me, sir?

**Tom**    I will, sir. The King.

**Northerton**    The King (**Tom** *takes a sip but* **Northerton** *drains.* **Tom** *does likewise and* **Northerton** *refills their mugs.*) Name's Northerton, the King's Third foot.

**Tom**    Tom Jones, at your service, sir.

**Northerton**    May I ask you where you are bound for, Mr Jones?

**Tom**    Well, I was heading for Bristol but I find I was given erroneous directions so now find myself heading for London. And you, sir, where are you bound for?

**Northerton**    Scotland, sir, to join my regiment. We are marching against the rebels and are expected to be commanded by the glorious Duke of Cumberland himself.

**Tom**    The Duke of Cumberland. (*A toast.*)

**Northerton**    The Duke of Cumberland.

*Once more* **Northerton** *drains his mug but* **Tom** *doesn't this time.* **Northerton** *notes this with a smirk when he goes to refill his mug.*

**Tom**    Well, sir, it should be a magnificent adventure.

**Northerton**    Oh, that indeed it will.

**Tom**    I am a man that suddenly finds himself at large in the world, in search of what life may have to offer him. I have a mind that I may like to take a commission in a regiment of the King's Army.

**Northerton**    Well, it's a fine life sir, if you have a mind to it. And it is an excellent choice for a gentleman adventurer.

**Tom**    Indeed.

**Northerton**    You are a gentleman, are you not, sir?

**Tom**    I toast you sir and wish you well in your fight for liberty and the Protestant religion.

**Northerton**    The Protestant religion? The Protestant religion? I fight not for no preaching parsons, sir. No, I'm in it strictly for the boozing, raping and mindless violence. In my opinion the parsons should fight their own battles.

**Tom**    I am sorry, sir, but I think no man can engage in a nobler cause than to fight for his beliefs.

**Northerton**    Uh, is this something you learnt from your university? (**Tom** *is silent.*) Which university did you attend, if I may ask sir?

**Tom**    Another toast. Mistress Sophia Weston.

**Northerton**    Sophia who?

**Tom**    Sophia Weston.

**Northerton**    Weston, Weston? Sophia Weston? There is only one Sophia Weston I've heard of and she has slept with half the young fellows in Bath – No, I shall not toast her, sir.

**Tom**    I am afraid you must be mistaken, sir, the Miss Weston I am talking of is a great lady of fashion and fortune.

**Northerton**    Aye, aye, and so is the one I'm talking of. Damn me she is notorious throughout the taverns in Bridges Street. She is small and fair-haired, with a huge . . . estate in Somersetshire. And she has an aunt.

**Tom**    Pray, sir, choose some other subject for your wit, for I promise I will bear no jesting with this lady's character.

**Northerton**   Jesting, damn me if Tom French of our regiment didn't have both her and her aunt in a bath in Bath.

**Mrs Waters** *comes out of her room and asks the* **Landlady** *something.*

**Tom**   You, sir, are one of the most impudent rascals upon earth.

**Northerton**   That's kind of you to say so. (*Spying* **Mrs Waters**.) Aha, there you are.

**Northerton** *leaps up from his chair and grabs her.*

**Mrs Waters**   Unhand me, sir.

**Northerton**   Once more unto the breach . . .

**Mrs Waters**   Sir, desist.

**Northerton**   Come on, love, it's time for military manouvres.

**Mrs Waters**   Geroff!

**Tom** *grabs* **Northerton**'*s shoulder and turns him around, but as he does the ensign sends him reeling with a headbutt.*

**Mrs Waters**   That is enough, sir.

**Tom** *recovers and gets the ensign in a headlock.*

**Tom**   You are not a gentleman, sir, I think I shall have words with your commanding officer about your conduct here.

**Northerton**   Zounds, sir, if you want her so badly then bloody have her.

**Tom** *releases him.*

**Tom**   For your affront to this lady and Miss Weston I shall have satisfaction of you, sir. Will you await my pleasure?

**Northerton**   Of course, sir.

**Northerton** *exits stage left.*

**Mrs Waters**    Oh, how can I thank you for my deliverance, Mister . . .?

**Tom**    Jones, madam, but I have done no more than would any other man.

**Mrs Waters**    Oh, sir, I could almost believe you to be some good angel than a man and, to say the truth, you look more like an angel than a man in my eye.

**Tom**    I have done no more than my duty in protecting you, ma'am.

**Mrs Waters**    I am indebted to you, sir, if I may repay you in some way.

**Tom**    It would please me if you joined me for supper.

**Mrs Waters**    It would be a pleasure, sir, but I have already ordered supper and it would be my honour if you joined me . . .

**Tom**    Certainly madam.

**Mrs Waters**    In my room.

**Tom**    Well, I . . .

**Mrs Waters**    Come, sir, don't be coy.

**Tom**    But . . .

**Mrs Waters**    I will insist, besides, do you really want to spend the night on the cold, hard floor?

**Tom**    Well, as you put it like that. But first, madam, I have some unfinished business. (**Tom** *turns to the door but* **Mrs Waters** *takes his hand and leads him towards her room.*) Madam I must . . . I should . . . Oh, well. But first . . . (**Tom** *goes to the door and looks out.*) Damn me the villain has made his escape.

**Tom** *and* **Mrs Waters** *exit into her room. A moment later* **Sophia** *and* **Mrs Honour**, *who is laden with luggage, enter.*

**Sophia**    Come along, Honour.

**Honour**    La madam, my legs are aching and my rump feels like it has been buggered by a troop of baboons. I could no longer sit on that horse as I could get off of it.

**Sophia**    Yes, it was nice of that stable boy to give you a hand down.

**Honour**    It was the hand up I was worried about.

**Sophia**    Well we should find a room here for the night and you can rest your . . .

**Mrs Fitzpatrick** *spots them, puts her book down and comes across to them.*

**Mrs Fitz**    Sophia, my dear, is that you?

**Sophia**    Harriet, my dear cousin, what a strange coincidence. What are you doing here?

*Air kisses.*

**Mrs Fitz**    More to the point, my dear, what are you doing here? It looks as if you are moving house.

**Sophia**    I have left the house of my overbearing father and make my way to London.

**Mrs Fitz**    So you could bear Uncle's blustering no more?

**Sophia**    Nor that of my aunt. They have requested, no ordered, that I marry a man that is abhorrent to me.

**Mrs Fitz**    Really, cousin, pray tell me, do I know the fellow?

**Sophia**    None other than Mr Blifil.

**Mrs Fitz**    Not that horrible spotty nephew of Mr Allworthy?

**Sophia**    None other.

**Mrs Fitz**    Good Lord, Old Boiley Blifil.

**Sophia**    Yes, I'm afraid so.

**Mrs Fitz**    My dear child, I am not surprised you have run away. He is not a fitting match for any woman.

**Sophia**   There is more, cousin. I have fallen in love.

**Mrs Fitz**   Fallen in love? (*Aside.*) Oh, dear.

**Sophia**   Yes, with Mr Tom Jones.

**Mrs Fitz**   Tom Jones? Not Tom Jones the bast . . .

**Sophia**   Yes, him.

**Mrs Fitz**   Well I suppose he's the better of two evils. It is a good job you have left Somerset as there seems to be a distinct lack of men in that county. You shall come with me and we shall find you more interesting conquests for you in London.

**Sophia**   But I want no other, I'm in love with Mr Jones.

**Mrs Fitz**   Oh, my dear child, we'll soon cure you of that.

**Sophia**   Are you going to London then?

**Mrs Fitz**   Yes, my dear.

**Sophia**   And Mr Fitzpatrick?

**Mrs Fitz**   Do not mention that man's name. A more loathsome creature hath not crawled from the Devil's backside. No sooner had we been married than he carried me off to his dreary estate in Cork.

**Sophia**   Oh dear.

**Mrs Fitz**   I was left alone whilst he went out drinking and carousing to the early hours with his friends. It turns out he was almost penniless and had only married me for my fortune. I became sick of his drunkenness and violent temper – and my dear he did have a temper. So I resolved to leave him and that dreadful place and return to London. My dear, Ireland is the most dismal place, and the people, oh don't ask me about the people. Everything is wet and grey. The people, the country, even the food.

**Honour** (*Pointedly at* **Mrs Fitzpatrick**.)   La, ma'am, can we find our rooms. We have barely rested for these last two nights and I am fit to drop.

**Mrs Fitz**   Oh, my dears, how inconsiderate of me, you must stay in my rooms tonight. Come I will show you the way.

**Sophia**   Oh, that will be wonderful, Harriot, we can be up early in the morning and continue our journey together. Come along Honour.

**Honour** (*Struggling off with bags*.)   Oh, la madam.

*They retire to* **Mrs Fitzpatrick**'s *room. Just as they exit* **Mr Fitzpatrick** *and* **Weston** *enter. They are obviously drunk.*

**Weston**   This is number six.

**Fitzpatrick**   No, this is the seventh.

**Weston**   No six.

**Fitzpatrick**   No seven.

**Weston**   Six.

**Fitzpatrick**   Seven.

**Weston**   All fat lasses come from Devon (*laughs*).

**Fitzpatrick**   What? Where is everybody? Landlord, drink.

*The* **Landlady** *appears.*

**Landlady**   What can I do for you gentlemen?

**Weston**   We'll come to that later, my pretty, first of all we want a drink.

**Fitzpatrick**   Drink.

*She produces two flagons and a jug of ale.* **Weston** *pours one flagon and passes it to* **Fitzpatrick**, *toasts him with the jug, then drinks from it. They both finish and belch loudly.*

**Weston**   I tell ye, Fitzpatrick, it was a most convenient coincidence bumping into you.

**Fitzpatrick**    Was indeed. To think we are both in search of errant women.

**Weston** *refills* **Fitzpatrick***'s mug.*

**Weston**    Women.

**Fitzpatrick**    Women.

**Weston**    Can't live with them.

**Fitzpatrick**    Drink.

*They drink, and belch again.*

**Weston**    Right, next.

**Fitzpatrick**    Hang on, we've forgotten something.

**Weston**    We 'ave?

**Fitzpatrick**    Aye, we're looking for something.

**Weston**    We are?

**Fitzpatrick**    The women.

**Weston**    Oh, yes, the women.

**Fitzpatrick** (*To the* **Landlady**.)    Madam have you seen a woman here tonight, travelling to London. A lady with a pretence of refinement, but who is nothing more than a low-grade whore. I have been catching her already in two or three places.

**Weston**    I've nearly caught many a woman in two or three places.

**Fitzpatrick**    If she be in the house, carry me up in the dark and show her to me, and if she be gone away before me, tell me which way to go after her, and I shall make thee the richest poor woman in this room.

**Fitzpatrick** *takes out a purse and they look conspiratorially around the room.*

**Landlady**   Oh sir, I couldn't (*He rattles the purse and she takes it and puts it down her cleavage.*) Well there is a lady of that description, but I saw her retire with a young gentleman.

**Fitzpatrick**   The slut. I'll whip her within an inch of her life.

**Landlady**   This way, sir.

*They creep towards the door in through which* **Tom** *and* **Mrs Waters** *disappeared.* **Weston** *sits down and helps himself to another drink. The sounds of giggling can be heard inside the room.* **Fitzpatrick** *kicks in the door and bursts in.*

**Fitzpatrick** (*O/S*)   I have you, you whore.

**Mrs Waters** (*O/S*)   Rape! Murder! Robbery! Rape!

**Tom** *runs out with just a sheet wrapped around him with* **Fitzpatrick** *on his tail and runs into* **Weston**.

**Weston**   Tom bastard Jones. We have the dog fox, I warrant the bitch is not far off.

*A comical chase ensues on and off stage until* **Weston** *and* **Fitzpatrick** *stop centre stage to catch their breath.*

**Weston**   Why are you chasing him?

**Fitzpatrick**   That villain hath debauched my wife and has got into bed with her.

**Weston**   Your wife! My niece! Why he's going for the full set, the little bastard.

**Weston** *runs off after* **Tom**. *Just then* **Mrs Fitzpatrick** *pokes her head out of her door and sees* **Fitzpatrick** *but he does not see her.*

**Mrs Fitz**   Oh, my lord, my husband.

*She slams the door shut. Just then* **Mrs Waters** *looks out of her door sees* **Fitzpatrick**, *screams and disappears back inside and slams the door.*

**Fitzpatrick**   That was not my wife.

**Tom** *runs across the stage with* **Weston** *close behind him.*

**Fitzpatrick**    Here, hang on a minute.

**Fitzpatrick** *runs after them off stage.* **Mrs Fitzpatrick** *opens her door again, checks the coast is clear, then emerges with* **Sophia** *and* **Honour***, who is laden with the luggage again.*

**Mrs Fitz**    Quickly cousin, if he should find me here there will be hell to pay.

**Sophia**    Come along Honour.

**Honour**    Yes ma'am.

*As they exit* **Honour** *drops* **Sophia***'s muff.*

**Tom** *reappears, stops to take his breath, and spots* **Sophia***'s muff.*

**Tom**    My Sophia's muff. (*He picks it up and puts it to his nose.*) I recognise the scent. How did it come to be here? Sophy was here – oh, my God. She could have seen . . . She must have seen . . .

**Weston** *and* **Fitzpatrick** *enter again.*

**Weston**    My daughter's muff, he is eating my daughter's muff. Bear witness the goods are found upon him. (*Grabbing* **Tom***.*) Where is my daughter villain?

**Tom**    Sir, I . . .

**Weston**    Is this not her muff?

**Tom**    Sir, the muff I acknowledge is the young lady's, but upon my honour I have not seen her.

**Fitzpatrick**    Upon my conscience, sir, you may be ashamed of denying your having seen the gentleman's daughter before my face, when you know I found you there upon the bed together.

**Weston**    My daughter? But I thought it was your wife.

**Fitzpatrick**    No, your daughter.

**Weston**    My daughter.

**Fitzpatrick**   Yes, your daughter

**Weston**   Not your wife.

**Fitzpatrick**   No, your daughter.

**Weston**   The bitch.

**Weston** *and* **Fitzpatrick** *burst into* **Mrs Waters'** *room again. A scream is heard, a crash and they both burst out again.*

**Weston**   That is not my daughter.

**Fitzpatrick**   Not your daughter?

**Weston**   Definitely not – and not your wife?

**Fitzpatrick**   No, not my wife.

*They both grin to themselves. Turn to go back into the room, catch each other and stop.*

**Weston**   Hang on a minute, that bitch of mine could still be in this house somewhere. Sophia, where are you?

**Weston** *exits in search of her.*

**Tom** *squares up to* **Fitzpatrick**.

**Tom**   Sir, a word if you please.

**Fitzpatrick**   Now, I can explain. Sir, you see . . .

*They both disappear off stage. A punch is heard,* **Fitzpatrick** *yelps, then* **Tom** *comes back on and gently knocks at* **Mrs Waters'** *door.*

**Tom**   It's me, Tom.

*The door opens and his clothes are flung out. He picks them up and runs off.* **Weston** *and* **Fitzpatrick** *reappear.*

**Weston**   She has escaped me again, damn the slut. Here, what happened to you?

**Fitzpatrick**   That scoundrel Jones caught me when my back was turned.

**Weston**   Where is the bastard?

**Fitzpatrick**  He ran off.

**Weston**  I'fackin bitch. And I have lost yet another morning for hunting, and it is confounded hard to lose one of the best days for scenting. Damn her and damn him. Ostler, fetch my horse.

*He exits and just as he does* **Mrs Waters** *appears at her door.*

**Fitzpatrick**  Madam I wish to apologise for my error.

**Mrs Waters**  I may have over reacted, sir. I am not used to having so many men in my room, well not all at once anyway.

**Fitzpatrick**  May I offer you a drink?

**Mrs Waters**  I am not dressed for such a thing.

**Fitzpatrick**  May I be so bold as to suggest I bring a bottle to your room?

**Mrs Waters**  Well, sir, you know where it is.

**Fitzpatrick**  I do indeed.

*She retreats back into her room,* **Fitzpatrick** *picks up a bottle and follows.*

*Blackout.*


### Scene Two – Lady Bellaston's House

*The lights come up on a well-appointed London town house.*

**Fielding**  So, thoughtfully fingering Sophia's muff Tom sets off again on the road to London. On arrival he finds lodgings at the house of Mrs Miller, where he and Mr Allworthy had stayed on the previous trips to the city. He immediately sent her young son, Bob, out in search of his beloved, and the young lad discovered that she and Mrs Fitzpatrick were staying at the house of a Lady Bellaston who, as it happens, was another, distant relation of the Weston family. Lady Bellaston was a notorious woman of society who reputedly entertained an entire company of guardsmen one night – with their horses. Having discovered where Sophia was staying Tom immediately paid the house a visit on pretence of returning her muff.

**Lady Bellaston** *and* **Mrs Fitzpatrick** *enter as* **Fielding** *exits.*

**Lady Bell**   Then you have seen this terrible man, madam? Pray is he so fine a figure as he is represented?

**Mrs Fitz**   Oh, Lady Bellaston, he is a man of curious good looks, but I'll warrant of hidden perversions and lust.

**Lady Bell**   Perversions, (*interested*) oh dear. And he is known for this throughout the county?

**Mrs Fitz**   It is said that he hath got nearly every gal in Somersetshire on her back at some time.

**Lady Bell**   Well that, my dear, is easy enough.

**Mrs Fitz**   But it is said that he is merciless. It is said that he chases them and, upon catching them, rips their clothes asunder and forces his attentions upon them.

**Both** (*Excited.*)   Oh, dear.

**Lady Bell**   And you say darling Sophia is in love with this person?

**Mrs Fitz**   Indeed madam, this is a matter of great consequence, for I believe that he may also be in love with her.

**Lady Bell**   Well we'll soon out a stop to that.

**Mrs Fitz**   We will?

**Lady Bell**   I shall be very glad to have my share in the preservation of a young lady of so much merit and for whom I have so much esteem. We shall ensure that a ditch is dug between them, this saving Miss Sophia and allowing Jones to pursue women that are more, how shall we say, receptive to his charms.

**Mrs Fitz**   We should send word to my uncle and acquaint him where my cousin is.

**Lady Bell**   That would be our duty.

**Mrs Honour** *enters*.

**Mrs Honour**   Ma'am, Mr Jones is here.

**Lady Bell**   Ah, really, well show him in. This is a lucky coincidence, now I get a chance to see the young fox for myself.

**Mrs Honour** *shows* **Tom** *in and exits*.

**Tom**   Lady Bellaston, Mrs Fitzpatrick, please forgive the intrusion but I have some urgent business with Miss Weston.

**Mrs Fitz**   Urgent, how urgent?

**Tom**   It concerns her muff.

**Lady Bell** (*Aside*.)   Good Lord, he gets straight to the point doesn't he?

**Mrs Fitz**   You may leave the article with me and I shall make sure she gets it.

**Tom**   I should prefer to give it to her myself.

**Lady Bell** (*Aside*.)   I bet you would.

**Mrs Fitz**   I am afraid that Miss Weston is not at home at the moment, but if you would like to aquaint Mrs Honour with your lodgings in London I will send for you at a more convenient time.

**Tom**   Thank you madam, you are most kind. With your permission I shall take my leave and wait with great expectation for your messenger. Your servant, madam, Lady Bellaston.

**Mrs Fitz**   Mr Jones.

**Tom** *exits*.

**Lady Bell**   He is rather young and ardent isn't he?

**Mrs Fitz**   Yes his breeches were rather tight, weren't they?

**Lady Bell**   I think it is our duty, madam, to rescue poor Sophia from his clutches. We must occupy her mind with some other diversions.

**Mrs Fitz**   Indeed so, but what?

**Lady Bell**   I believe I know of such a gentleman that can help us.

**Mrs Fitz**   Really, please tell me more.

**Lady Bell**   All in good time, my dear, all in good time.

*Blackout.*


### Scene Three – Vauxhall Gardens, a masked ball

*The stage is festooned with lights, there is music and couples dancing. Amongst them* **Fielding** *appears.*

**Fielding**   Now Tom waited impatiently for two days for news from Mrs Fitzpatrick then a parcel arrived. It contained a fine suit of clothes and ticket for a masked ball here at Vauxhall Gardens. Within the parcel was a card. It said to Mr Jones, the Queen of the Fairies sends you this, use her favours not amiss. Excitedly Jones got ready for his rendezvous, hoping at last to meet again with his fair Sophia.

**Tom** *enters followed at a discreet distance by* **Lady Bellaston**. *He goes to talk to a young lady but* **Lady Bellaston** *touches him on the shoulder.*

**Lady Bell**   If you talk any longer with that trollop I will acquaint Miss Weston.

**Tom**   Madam, you know her? Is she here? Please madam, answer me, is she here?

**Lady Bell**   Hush, sir, you will be observed. I promise you, upon my honour, Miss Weston is not here.

**Tom**   Then please, I entreat you, tell me where she is, Mrs Fitzpatrick. Indeed my good Fairy Queen, I know your majesty well, even though you disguise your voice.

**Lady Bell**   You have discovered me, sir, but I will keep this affection in my voice so as not to be discovered by others. Good sir, I am afraid I cannot assist in carrying on an affair between you and my cousin, which I fear must end in her ruin as well as your own. Besides my cousin is not so mad as to consent to her own destruction, unless you are so much her enemy as to tempt her to it.

**Tom**   You know not my heart if you call me the enemy of Sophia.

**Lady Bell**   To ruin anyone is the act of an enemy. Now, sir, my cousin hath very little more than her father would please to give her, very little for one of her fashion. You know him and you know your own situation.

**Tom**   My love is not the base thing that would see her ruined to achieve its own satisfaction. I would sacrifice everything to the possession of my Sophia but Sophia herself.

**Lady Bell**   Oh, very good. Is that a line you use with many women? I am convinced that it may work with some.

**Tom**   I hope I have not offended . . .

**Lady Bell**   Are you so little versed in our sex to try and woo a lady by entertaining her with your passion for another woman?

**Tom**   I'm sorry . . .

**Lady Bell**   Come, Mr Jones, do not act the innocent with me. The Fairy Queen can see right through you.

**Tom**   Madam I am afraid . . .

**Lady Bell**   Oh, don't be afraid, sir. I am prepared to sacrifice myself to you for the sake of the family.

**Tom**   Why, madam, do I understand that you require my bottom to your Titania?

**Lady Bell**   I want more than your bottom. (*She kisses him passionately.*)

**Tom**   Madam, you have taken me unawares.

**Lady Bell**   Really, I don't wear any myself.

**Tom** *unmasks her.*

**Tom**   Good Lord, Lady Bellaston.

**Lady Bell**   Mr Jones.

**Tom**   Oh, Lady Bellaston.

*She takes him off stage.*


### Scene Four – Lady Bellaston's House

*The lights come up on* **Fielding**. *As he speaks* **Tom** *and* **Lady Bellaston** *enter – they are all over each other.*

**Fielding**   And thus Lady Bellaston begins the seduction of Tom Jones. Over the next week or so they met several times. Tom tried to refuse the invitations but was lured to the trap with hope of news of his darling Sophia. Towards the end, however, he rarely remembered to mention her name. All hope of seeing her again had disappeared from Tom's heart. One night Lady Bellaston brought the young man back to her house, after first ensuring that the servants had the night off and Sophie was being entertained at the theatre by one of Lady Bellaston's many friends, a Lord Fellamar.

**Lady Bell**   Wait here, my darling, I am just going to freshen up.

**Lady Bellaston** *exits.*

**Sophia** (*O/S*)   No, my Lord Fellamar, I am very tired and all I desire is my bed. No, no, no it was a lovely evening. Yes it was unfortunate about the play. No, I've never been in a riot before. Yes, we must do it again some time. No, no, not the riot. Well, goodnight, my lord. Yes, yes, goodnight. Goodnight.

**Sophia** *enters and sees* **Tom**.

**Tom**   I see madam that you are surprised.

**Sophia**   Oh, heavens indeed, I am surprised. I almost doubt you are the person you seem.

**Tom**   Indeed, madam, I am. Oh, my darling Sophia, if only you knew the thousand torments I have suffered in this fruitless pursuit.

**Sophia**   Pursuit of whom?

**Tom**   How can you be so cruel to ask that question? Need I say of you?

**Sophia**   Of me? Hath Mr Jones then such important business with me?

**Tom**   To some, madam, this might seem an important business.

*He takes her muff from his coat and hands it to her.*

I found it at the inn at Upton. It has not left my side ever since.

**Sophia**   My muff . . . Upton?

**Tom**   Let us not, I beseech you, lose one of those precious moments which fortune hath so kindly sent us. Oh, my Sophia, I have business of a much superior kind. Thus, on my knees, let me ask your pardon.

**Sophia**   Pardon?

**Tom**   I scarce know what to say. By heavens I scarce wish you would pardon me. Oh, my Sophia, my love, you cannot hate me for what happened at Upton more than I do myself. She whose company I accidentally fell is not an object of serious love. Believe me, my angel, I have never seen her from that day to this.

**Sophia**   Haven't seen whom?

**Tom**   Sorry?

**Sophia**   Who is it you have not seen since Upton?

**Tom**   Ah, I thought you . . . didn't you . . . well I. It is of little consequence. My darling I love you. I am on my knees and prepared to swear to stand by you till death us do part.

**Sophia**   Oh Tom, I cannot. Duty to my father forbids me to follow my own inclinations. But ruin with you would be more welcome to me than the most affluent fortune with another man.

**Tom**   I cannot ruin thee. I will renounce you, give you up. Oh, Sophy my love I will ever retain but it shall be at a distance from you. It shall be in some foreign land, from whence no voice, no sign of despair, shall ever reach and disturb your ears. And when I am dead . . .

**Sophia** *puts her finger to his lips.*

**Sophia**   My darling Tom.

**Tom**   Oh Sophia.

*They are about to kiss when* **Sophia** *suddenly pulls away.*

**Sophia**   One moment, how did you get here?

**Tom**   Ah.

**Lady Bellaston** *enters and they quickly pull apart.*

**Lady Bell**   I thought, Miss Weston, you had been at the play?

**Sophia**   The audience found the content unpalatable so drew it to an abrupt conclusion.

**Lady Bell**  They walked out?

**Sophia**  No, they stormed the stage, lynched the cast, and put the theatre to the torch.

**Lady Bell**  Oh dear, everyone's a critic nowadays. I should not have broken in on you so abruptly had I known you had company.

**Sophia**  But I . . . ? I assure you madam that . . .

**Lady Bell**  I hope at least I interrupt no business.

**Sophia**  No madam, our business is at an end.

**Lady Bell**  That was quick.

**Sophia**  I had lost my muff and this gentleman was kind enough to return it to me.

**Lady Bell**  Miss Weston, you are fortunate indeed to have these things returned. It is lucky that they landed in the hands of a gentleman. One finds if a baser fellow gets hold of one's muff it is very difficult to get his hands off of it. And how did you know who it belonged to, sir?

**Tom**  Er . . . there was a note inside the muff.

**Lady Bell**  A muff with a message, how odd.

**Tom**  I believe madam it is customary to give some reward on these occasions.

**Lady Bell**  A reward, sir?

**Tom**  Yes, and I must insist on a very high one for my honesty. It is, madam, no less than the honour of being permitted to pay another visit here.

**Lady Bell**  I make no doubt that you are a gentleman, and my doors are never shut to men of fashion.

**Tom**  Thank you madam, but now it is late and with your permission I will take my leave.

**Lady Bell**    Indeed, sir, and I look forward to our next meeting.

**Tom**    Ladies.

**Tom** *exits with a deep bow.*

**Lady Bell**    Upon my word a good and pretty young fellow. I do not remember seeing his face before.

**Sophia**    Nor I, madam. I must say he behaved very handsomely.

**Lady Bell**    Yes, and he is a very handsome fellow, don't you think?

**Sophia**    I did not take much notice of him.

**Lady Bell**    You must forgive me my dear, for when I came into the room I had a suspicion that he was your Mr Jones himself.

**Sophia**    Did your ladyship indeed.

**Lady Bell**    Yes, I vow I did. I can't imagine what put it into my head for, to give the fellow his due, he was genteelly dressed, which I think, dear Sophy, is not commonly the case with your friend.

**Sophia**    Your raillery is a little cruel, Lady Bellaston.

**Lady Bell**    You think so?

**Sophia**    I have promised you I will not marry without my father's consent.

**Lady Bell**    That is why the raillery is not cruel, because what has passed is past. If you cannot bear a little ridicule I shall begin to fear you are very far gone indeed, and almost question whether you have dealt ingenuously with me.

**Sophia**    Indeed madam, your ladyship mistakes me. I have not given any thought to Mr Jones.

**Lady Bell**   You had said Mr Jones was a fellow of rare good looks.

**Sophia**   I thought your ladyship had allowed him to be handsome?

**Lady Bell**   Whom pray?

**Sophia**   Mr Jones – no, no, I mean the gentleman who was just now here.

**Lady Bell**   Sophy, Sophy, Sophy, this Mr Jones still runs in your head.

**Sophia**   Upon my honour, madam, Mr Jones is as entirely indifferent to me as . . . as . . . as the gentleman who just left us.

**Lady Bell**   Yes, I believe you.

**Sophia** *picks up her muff and holds it to her nose then remembers herself.*

**Sophia**   Goodnight madam.

**Lady Bell**   Goodnight my dear Sophia.

**Sophia** *exits.* **Fielding** *enters.*

**Fielding**   Now, Lady Bellaston saw Sophie as a rival for young Tom's affections. It is not that she wanted to keep Tom for herself, oh no, Lady Bellaston is a woman of society and she hunts men as a country gentleman hunts the fox; and if there is another Diana bearing down upon her quarry she will try, by both fair means and foul, to put her off the scent. So the following morning (**Sophia** *enters reading a book and sits*) she puts her terrier to the sport.

**Lord Fellamar** *enters.*

**Fielding** *exits.*

**Fellamar**   Lady Bellaston, it is hard to believe that this blazing star is the daughter of a country booby squire. Upon my soul, I should swear she had been bred in a court for, besides her beauty, I ain't never saw anything so genteel, so sensible, so polite. Upon my honour I am in love with her to distraction.

**Lady Bell**   You do yourself no great ill either, Lord Fellamar, for she is an only child and her father's estate is a good £3000 a year.

**Fellamar**   Then I can assure you, madam, I think her the best match in all England.

**Lady Bell**   Indeed, my lord, if you like her then you shall have her.

**Fellamar**   Then, as you are related madam, will you do me the honour of proposing me to her father.

**Lady Bell**   Are you really then in earnest?

**Fellamar**   Madam, I would not jest with your ladyship in an affair of this kind.

**Lady Bell**   I will indeed then readily propose your lordship to her father, and I can assure you of his joyful acceptance of the proposal, but alas . . .

**Fellamar**   What?

**Lady Bell**   You have a rival, my lord.

**Fellamar**   Upon my word, madam, you have struck a damp to my heart and almost deprived me of being.

**Lady Bell**   I should rather have hoped I had struck a fire in you.

**Fellamar**   Pray, madam, who is this happy man?

**Lady Bell**   One of the lowest fellows in the world. He is a beggar, a bastard, a foundling, a fellow in meaner circumstance as one of your footmen.

**Fellamar**   Is it possible that a young creature of such perfections should think of bestowing herself so unworthily?

**Lady Bell**   It is the country living, my lord, it softens
the brain.

**Fellamar**   Such ruin as this must be prevented.

**Lady Bell**   My lord, how can it be prevented, the family
have done all in their power. The girl is intoxicated, nothing
less than ruin will content her.

**Fellamar**   Has her ladyship tried reasoning with her?

**Lady Bell**   My dear lord, you know better than to try
reasoning with a young woman out of her inclinations.

**Fellamar**   What is to be done?

**Lady Bell**   Nothing but violent methods will do.

**Fellamar**   Violent methods?

**Lady Bell**   If your lordship really hath this attachment to
my cousin. I think there may be one way. Indeed it is a very
disagreeable one. It requires great spirit, I promise you.

**Fellamar**   I am not, madam, conscious of any defect there,
nor am I, I hope, suspected of any such.

**Lady Bell**   Of course not. No, no, I can't – I can't bear the
apprehension of it.

**Fellamar**   Come, madam, I am unanimous in this.

**Lady Bell**   It must not be.

**Fellamar**   Madam, I insist.

**Lady Bell**   Very well – you must take her by force.

**Fellamar**   Force? Well I, I am not sure that . . .

**Lady Bell**   Fie upon it, sir, are you frightened of the word
rape? Remember the story of the Sabine women?

**Fellamar**   Well, I . . .

**Lady Bell**　It is said that they made tolerable good wives afterwards. I fancy a few of my married acquaintances were ravished by their husbands.

**Fellamar**　Madam . . .

**Lady Bell**　My lord, I betray my sex most abominably. All women love a man of spirit. Within a few hours she may be in the arms of one who surely doth not deserve her, though I give him his due, I believe he is truly a man of spirit.

**Fellamar**　I hope so, madam, for within that time she shall be mine.

**Lady Bell**　Well spoken, my lord. Within this week I am convinced I shall call your lordship cousin in public.

**Lady Bellaston** *exits and* **Fellamar** *approaches* **Sophia**.

**Fellamar**　I am afraid, Miss Weston, I break in upon you abruptly.

**Sophia**　Indeed, my Lord Fellamar, I am myself surprised at this unexpected visit.

**Fellamar**　If this visit be unexpected, madam, my eyes must have been very faithless interpreters of my heart when last I had the honour of seeing you, for surely you could not otherwise have hoped to detain my heart in your possession without recieving a visit from its owner.

**Sophia**　I am sorry, my lord, I do not understand . . .

**Fellamar**　You shall want no longer, my darling Sophia, you may have me – I am all yours.

*He grabs her hand and starts kissing it.*

**Sophia**　My lord, are you out of your senses?

**Fellamar**　I am indeed, madam, and sure you will pardon the effects of a frenzy of which you yourself have occasioned, for love hath totally deprived me of reason that I am scarce accountable for any of my actions.

**Sophia**   I shall not stay to hear any more of this.

**Fellamar**   Do not think of leaving me thus cruelly. Could you know half the torments I feel, that tender bosom must pity what those eyes have caused. You are, you must, you shall be mine.

**Sophia**   Sir, if you do not desist, I will raise the family.

**Fellamar**   You have already raised more than that.

*He leaps upon her.*

**Weston** (*O/S*)   Damn me I'll unkennel her this instant. Show me to her chamber I say. Where is my daughter? I know she's in this house and I'll see her if she's above ground. Show me where she is. (**Weston** *enters followed by* **Mrs Fitzpatrick**.) There you are – ye gods, another one, she's like a bitch on heat. Every damned dog from here to bloody Jerusalem is sniffing round her. What is it with you, madam, can ye not keep yer legs together for five minutes?

**Fellamar** *drops* **Sophia**, *stands up and adjusts himself.*

**Mrs Fitz**   For heaven's sake, Uncle, mitigate your wrath. You are in the house of a great lady. You should be satisfied that you have found your daughter.

**Weston**   Yes, I have found the bitch, but it may be too late. It is no good to shut the stable door when the horse has bolted, and this one looks like it's had a troop of cavalry through it.

**Sophia**   Oh Father, it was not how it seemed.

**Weston**   Not how it seemed, not how it seemed? Look, I'll forgive ye if you wilt have him. If wilt have him Sophy I'll forgive ye all. Why dost unt speak? Shat ha'un? Damn me shat ha'un? Why dost unt answer? Was ever such a stubborn toad.

**Mrs Fitz**   Let me entreat you, Uncle, to be a little more moderate. You frighten the girl so that you deprive her of all power of utterance.

**Weston**   Power of mine arse. You take her part then do you? You side with an undutiful child.

**Mrs Fitz**   No, I . . .

**Lady Bellaston** *enters.*

**Weston**   There, my lady cousin, stands the most undutiful child in the world. She hankers after a beggarly rascal and won't marry one of the greatest matches in all England.

**Lady Bell**   Indeed, Cousin Weston, I am persuaded you wrong my cousin. I am sure she hath a better understanding. I am convinced she will not refuse what she must be sensible is so much to her advantage.

**Weston**   Do you hear there what her ladyship says? All your family are for the match. Come Sophy, be a good girl and be dutiful and make your father happy.

**Sophia**   If my death will make you happy, sir, it will shortly be so.

**Weston**   It's a lie, Sophy, it's a damned lie and you know it.

**Lady Bell**   Indeed, Miss Weston, you injure your father. He had nothing in view but your interest in this match, and I and all your friends must acknowledge the highest honour done to your family in the proposal.

**Weston**   Aye, all of us. Come, Sophy, let me beg you once more to be a good girl and give me your consent before your cousin.

**Lady Bellaston** *takes hold of* **Fellamar**'s *arm.*

**Lady Bell**   Let me give him your hand, cousin, it is the fashion nowadays to dispense with time and long courtships.

**Weston**   Aye, they'll have time enough to court afterwards. People may court very well after they have been abed together.

**Fellamar**   Though I have not the honour, sir, of being personally known to you, yet as I find I have the happiness of having my proposal accepted let me intercede, sir, on behalf of the young lady, that she may not be more solicited at this time.

**Weston**   You intercede, sir? Why, who the devil are you?

**Fellamar**   Sir, I am Lord Fellamar. I am the happy man whom I hope you have done the honour of accepting as a son-in-law.

**Weston**   You are a son of a bitch for all your laced coat. You, my son-in-law, be damned to you.

**Fellamar**   I shall take more from you, sir, than from any other man but I must inform you that I am not used to hear such language without resentment.

**Weston**   Resent my arse.

**Fellamar**   Sir, I am willing to impute everything down to the effect of liquor, and the most trifling acknowledgement to that kind will set everything right. For I have the most violent attachment to your daughter and, you sir, are the last person upon earth whom I would resent an affront. I wish to put the entire affair behind us without any imputation on my honour. All I desire, sir, is that you make some acknowledgement, however slight, so that I pay me respects to you in order to obtain your leave to visit the young lady on the footing of a lover.

**Weston**   Say that again?

**Fellamar**   Your daughter, sir . . .

**Weston**   The girl is disposed of already.

**Fellamar**   Perhaps, sir, you are not sufficiently apprised of the greatness of this offer. I believe such a person, title and fortune would be nowhere refused.

**Weston**   Lookee, sir, to be very plain my daughter is bespoke already, but if she was not I would not marry her to no lord on no account. I hate all lords. They are a parcel of Hanovarians and I will have nothing to do with them. Do not think I am afraid of such a fellow as thee art. I'll teach you to father-in-law me, I'll lick thy jacket.

**Weston** *gives* **Fellamar** *a prod.*

**Fellamar**   Well, sir, then I will desire your company at Hyde Park tomorrow morning.

**Weston**   I cannot, sir, I am busy.

**Fellamar**   You will not refuse me satisfaction, sir.

**Weston**   Satisfaction! Satisfaction! Is that how you want it? (**Weston** *takes up boxing stance.*) I'll take a bout with thee. I'll box thee for a bellyful.

**Fellamar**   It is very well sir that I'll make no disturbance before the ladies.

**Weston**   Come on, put them up.

**Fellamar**   I see, sir, you are below my notice. (*To* **Lady Bellaston**.) I am afraid, madam, I will have to take my leave. Lady Bellaston, your humble servant.

**Fellamar** *bows and exits.*

**Weston**   Come back 'ere and fight you bastard. Come back 'ere. Who the bloody hell was he anyway?

**Lady Bell**   Bless me, sir, you have affronted a nobleman of the first rank and fortune who has made proposals to your daughter.

**Weston**   I will have nothing to do with any of your lords. My daughter shall have an honest country gentleman. I have pitched on one for her and she shall have 'un. Come, madam, you must along with me. (*Throws* **Sophia** *over his shoulder.*) Shat 'ave im, damn me shat 'ave im.

*Exit* **Weston** *then, after a moment,* **Mrs Fitzpatrick** *and* **Lady Bellaston**.

*Blackout.*


## Scene Five – Tom's Lodgings

*Lights come up on a modest room – a couple of chairs and a table.* **Fielding** *is stood stage right.*

**Fielding**   So, the bitch has been kennelled again – as the squire would put it – but this time in the squire's London lodgings, which falls well for Lady Bellaston who continues her seduction of young Tom.

**Tom** *enters musing over a letter.*

**Tom**   You, sir, are a man of the world are you not?

**Fielding**   I like to think so, sir.

**Tom**   Then maybe you could assist me in a small problem I have.

**Fielding**   If it is within my means, sir, I will be happy to.

**Tom**   I have recently engaged in a relationship with a woman with whom I am so entangled with I know not how to extricate myself.

**Fielding**   Are you in love, sir?

**Tom**   In love? No, more like entrapped, and I am under obligations to her. How can I possibly desert such a woman?

**Fielding**   Would this person be a Lady Bellaston?

**Tom**   Yes, it would. How do you know, sir?

**Fielding**   Let's just say that I do. I also know that she is a remarkably liberal lady and enjoys her freedom so that she may pursue other young gentlemen such as yourself. There is only one method to dispose of such a woman.

**Tom**   What is that, sir?

**Fielding**   You must propose marriage.

**Tom**   Marriage?

**Fielding**   Aye, marriage.

**Tom**   But . . .

**Fielding**   I guarantee, sir, that she will declare it off in a moment.

**Tom**   And if she should take me at my word, where am I then? Caught in my own trap.

**Fielding**   Trust me, it won't come to that. If it does we will think of an answer to that problem too. Have you paper and pen?

**Tom**   I have, sir.

**Fielding**   Then lead on, sir.

*Blackout.*

*A spotlight comes up on* **Lady Bellaston** *reading a letter.*

**Lady Bell**   Marriage? How dare he?

**Lord Fellamar** *enters.*

**Fellamar**   That man is insufferable.

**Lady Bell**   Who?

**Fellamar**   Darling Sophy's father.

**Lady Bell**   He is not your problem. He can be won over, if we can manage to catch him sober. No the only danger lies in the fellow I have formerly mentioned (*fingering the letter*) who has, by some means or other, I know not what, procured himself tolerable clothes and passes for a gentleman. I have made it my business to enquire after this fellow and I have luckily found out his lodgings. I am thinking, my lord, that this fellow is far too mean for your personal resentment. Maybe you could devise some way for him to be pressed and put on board a ship?

**Fellamar** On board a ship – what a marvellous idea. I will send some men around there forthwith.

*He exits and is momentarily followed by* **Lady Bellaston** *under a flurry of naval music.*

*The lights come up on* **Tom**'s *lodgings again.* **Tom** *is dressing.*

*There is a knock at the door.*

**Tom** Come in. (**Mrs Honour** *enters.*) Mrs Honour?

**Mrs Honour** Oh sir, how shall I get spirits to tell you? You are undone, sir, and my poor lady's undone, and I am undone.

**Tom** Has anything happened to Sophia?

**Mrs Honour** All that is bad. Oh, I shall never get another lady. Oh, that I should live to see this day. Oh, Mr Jones I have lost my lady for ever.

**Tom** How? What? For heaven's sakes tell me. Oh, my dear Sophia.

**Mrs Honour** You may well call her so, she was the dearest lady to me. I shall never have another place.

**Tom** Damn your place, what has become of my Sophia?

**Mrs Honour** Aye, to be sure, servants may be damned. It signifies nothing of what becomes of them, though they are turned away and ruined ever so much. To be sure they are not flesh and blood like other people. No, to be sure, it signifies nothing what becomes of them.

**Mrs Honour** *starts to bawl.*

**Tom** I beg of you, tell me what has happened to my Sophia?

**Mrs Honour** I don't damn you because you have lost the sweetest lady in the world. To be sure, you are worthy to be pitied, but I am worthy to be pitied too. For to be sure, if ever there was a good mistress . . .

**Tom** Mrs Honour, please, what has happened?

**Mrs Honour** Why the worst thing that could have happened, her father has come to town and carried her away.

**Tom** Her father has carried her away? Is that it? Oh, thank God it was not worse.

**Mrs Honour** No worse? What could be worse for either of us? He carried her off swearing that she would marry Mr Blifil and I am turned out of doors for aiding her escape.

**Tom** True, Mrs Honour, it is bad, but you frightened me out of my wits. I feared much worse. Where there is life there is hope. Women in this land of liberty cannot be married by actual brute force.

**Mrs Honour** To be sure, sir, there may be some hopes for you but, alack a day, what hopes are there for poor me?

**Tom** I am sensible to my obligation to you and will make amends.

**Mrs Honour** What can make a servant amends for the loss of one place is the getting of another.

**Tom** We will find you a place but until then . . .

**N/O** You can't go up there ma'am.

**Mrs Fitz** (*N/O*) I've come to see Mr Jones.

**N/O** Sorry, ma'am, he is busy.

**Tom** Oh, good Lord . . .

**Mrs Honour**    What?

**Tom**    It's Mrs Fitzpatrick . . . quickly get in here . . .

**Tom** *hides* **Mrs Honour** *behind a door.*

**Mrs Honour**    But I . . .

**Tom**    No buts, she mustn't find you here. Now keep quiet.

*The door bursts open and* **Mrs Fitzpatrick** *enters.*

**N/O**    Oh, bugger.

**Tom**    Why, Mrs Fitzpatrick, this is an unexpected pleasure.

**Mrs Fitz**    I have come Mr Jones (*Beat.*) against my better
judgement, with grave news that I think is of some
importance to you. I have come of late to more fully
understand your character and your feelings for my dear
cousin.

**Tom**    Mrs Fitzpatrick I . . .

**Mrs Fitz**    No, please let me finish. These feelings I do
believe come from your heart and your intentions are truly
honourable. I think it is that my history compels me to
conclude, in the first instance, that you were some beggarly
knave set upon darling Sophia's inheritance. Now I see
differently. I pity you, Mr Jones, it is the curse of such
tenderness to be thrown away on those who are insensible of
it. I know my cousin better than you, Mr Jones, and I must
say any woman who makes no return to such a passion is
unworthy.

**Tom**    Madam, please . . .

**Mrs Fitz**    There is something in true tenderness
bewitching. Few women ever meet with it in men, and fewer
still no how to value it when they do.

**Tom**    Madam, I don't think . . .

**Mrs Fitz**    I know how to value it, Mr Jones. Oh, Mr Jones
you might at this instant sit for the picture of Adonis . . .

*She leaps on* **Tom**.

**Tom**   Oh God, not again.

*There is a crash from* **Honour**'s *hiding place.*

**Mrs Fitz**   Is this usage to be borne, Mr Jones, basest of men.
What wretch is this to whom you have exposed me?

**Mrs Honour**   Wretch? Wretch, forsooth, as poor a wretch
as I am I am honest, that is more than some folks who are
richer can say.

**Mrs Fitz**   Oh, Mrs Honour.

**Mrs Honour**   Oh, Mrs Fitzpatrick.

**Tom**   Oh, God.

*Enter* **Mr Fitzpatrick** *in a fury.*

**Mrs Fitz**   My husband.

**Tom**   Mr Fitzpatrick.

**Fitzpatrick**   There you are, you bitch, I thought if I
followed you long enough I'd find the bastard that had been
riding thee. Good God, it's you, the bastard from Upton. I'll
'ave satisfaction of thee.

**Fitzpatrick** *draws his sword.*

**Tom**   No, sir, please. I can explain. (**Fitzpatrick** *lunges at*
**Tom**.) Sir, this is folly.

**Fitzpatrick**   Defend yourself, sir.

*They scuffle during which* **Mrs Fitzpatrick** *and* **Mrs Honour**
*exit.* **Fitzpatrick** *accidentally stabs himself with his own sword and
falls to the floor.*

**Fitzpatrick**   I have satisfaction enough, I am a dead man.

**Tom**   I hope not, sir, but you have drawn it upon yourself.

*Two masked men rush in and seem surprised at what they find.*

**Man One**    A murder, a murder.

**Man Two**    Quickly, grab him.

*They take hold of* **Tom**.

**Tom**    Let go of me, I can explain . . .

**Man Two**    You'll do your explaining to the magistrate, boy.

**Man Two** *exits with* **Tom**. **Fitzpatrick** *groans.*

**Man One**    Oh, you still with us, sir? We best get ye to a surgeon.

*Blackout.*


### Scene Six – Allworthy's Lodging

*As modestly furnished as* **Tom**'s.

**Fielding** *enters.*

**Fielding**    The men that happened so conveniently upon the scene were none other than the press gang sent by Lord Fellamar. The captain of the band saw it was his duty to take poor Tom before the Justice. Members of the gang, themselves, testified as how they saw Tom set upon this unfortunate gentleman and the surgeon, who attended Mr Fitzpatrick, testified that the wound was indeed mortal. Tom was then committed to the gatehouse where he spent a sorry night in contemplation of the deed – for although it was not his fault he did not relish the taking of a life. A couple of days later Mr Allworthy (**Allworthy** *enters reading a letter*), accompanied by Mr Blifil, came to London on business.

**Fielding** *exits as* **Weston** *enters almost dragging* **Sophia**. *He sits her on a chair down stage.*

**Weston**    Ah, Allworthy, this is a fine business. The hounds have changed on us and when we thought we had a fox to deal with it turns out to be a badger.

**Allworthy**   Pray, good neighbour, drop your metaphors and speak a little plainer.

**Blifil** *enters excitedly, tries to say something but is cut off by* **Weston**.

**Weston**   Well I'll tell you plainly. We have been all this time been afraid of a son of a whore of a bastard of somebody's, but now we have a confounded son of a whore of a lord – who may be a bastard for ought I know or care – for he shall not have a daughter of mine by my consent. I shall pack Sophia back to the country tomorrow unless she consents to be married directly to Mr Blifil, and there she shall spend all her days in a garret upon bread and water; and the sooner such a bitch breaks her heart the better though, damn her, I believe she is too stubborn.

**Allworthy**   Please don't be hasty, my friend.

**Weston**   I was trapped in a room of women last night, and not the type of women you wanted to be trapped in a room with. There was Lady Bellaston, Lady Betty, Lady Catherine and my lady I-don't-know-who. Damn me if ever you catch me among such a kennel of hoop-petticoat bitches. 'Oh, certainly one of the greatest matches in all England', says one; 'A very advantageous offer', says another; 'Surely cousin', says that fat-arsed bitch Lady Bellaston, 'you must be out of your wits to think of refusing such an offer.'

**Allworthy**   Ah, now I begin to understand. Some person has made proposals to Miss Weston, which the ladies of the family approve but is not to your liking.

**Weston**   He is a lord and I am resolved to have nothing to do with them. Besides I have made a contract with you.

**Allworthy**   Ah, now, as to that matter; I entirely release you, sir, from any engagement, for no contract can be binding between parties who have not the full power to make it.

**Weston**   You what? I tell you I have the power and I will fulfill it.

**Allworthy**   I have thought on this matter, neighbour. Your daughter possesses many fine attributes . . .

**Blifil** (*aside*)   She does indeed.

**Allworthy**   Many fine attributes that will make her an excellent wife. I am in love with her character and would heartily wish to receive this jewel into our family. But, though I wish many good things, I would not steal them or be guilty of any violence or injustice to possess them, and I will not see this young lady forced into marriage, as I see her inclinations are averse to my nephew.

**Blifil**   But uncle . . .

**Weston**   Did I not beget her? Did I not beget her? Then allow me then to be her father. And, if I be, then am I not to govern my own child? And if I am to govern her in other matters am I not to govern her in this? And what is it that am I desiring all this while? Am I desiring for her to do anything for me? To give me anything? No, all I am desiring is for her to take away half my estate now and the other half when I die. And what's it all for? Why, isn't it to make her happy?

**Blifil**   I have read that women are seldom proof against perseverance, and with such perseverance I am sure at last I could gain those inclinations when, in the future, I shall not have a rival, but at the moment I am too sensible that that wickedest of men remains uppermost in her heart.

**Weston**   Aye, aye, so he does.

**Blifil**   But I expect, when she hears of the murder which he hath committed . . .

**Allworthy**   Murder?

**Sophia**   Tom hath committed a murder?

**Blifil**   Yes, a murder. (*Putting it to* **Allworthy**.) That Jones, that wretch whom you nourished at your bosom, hath proved to be one of the greatest villains on earth.

**Allworthy**   I can hardly believe it?

**Blifil**   It is true, he hath killed a man. A Mr Fitzpatrick.

**Weston**   Fitzpatrick?

**Blifil**   Yes, sir. He has killed a Mr Fitzpatrick. I will not say murdered, for perhaps it may not be so construed in the law, and I hope the best for his sake.

**Sophia**   Good Lord, how can this be?

**Weston**   I tell thee what, I have not heard better news in my life. He hath committed a murder. And there's hopes of seeing him hanged? Ha, ha. (*He starts to caper around the room.*) Now, what have you got to say about that, my girl?

**Mrs Waters** *enters.*

**Mrs Waters**   Mr Allworthy?

**Blifil** *turns swiftly when he hears her voice, takes her by the arm and tries to steer her off stage.*

**Blifil**   Ah madam, if you don't mind, it is not a convenient time, my uncle is extremely distressed.

**Mrs Waters**   But, I must see him. I insist. (*Pushes past* **Blifil**.) Mr Allworthy? Please forgive the intrusion, sir, but your landlady let me in. I have some important news. News that will bring you some solace concerning the person of Mr Jones.

**Allworthy**   What of that unfortunate boy? What is it that you have to tell me?

**Mrs Waters**   Before I speak, sir, may I ask you a question? Why is it that you are planning to prosecute Mr Jones for a murder he hath not committed?

**Allworthy**   What? I prosecute him. I have no idea what you are talking about . . . Not committed?

**Mrs Waters** The unfortunate Mr Fitzpatrick, whose murder Tom has been accused of, has been lodging with me during his recovery.

**Allworthy** Recovery?

**Mrs Waters** Yes, sir.

**Sophia** Oh, thank the Lord.

**Weston** Ahhh, nuts.

**Mrs Waters** I am afraid that the young surgeon that attended him was grievously mistaken. He assumed the effects of strong liquor to be the last breath of a mortally wounded man. I personally believe that it was the alcohol that preserved Mr Fitzpatrick. He is alive and well and currently drunk; but prior to this regular condition he hath sent word to the magistrate that not only is he alive but was also the instigator of the incident.

**Sophia** Where is Tom now?

**Mrs Waters** He is outside.

**Sophia** Outside?

**Weston** Oh, it just gets better.

**Mrs Waters** I took the liberty of bringing him here after his release, because there is more to tell you and he should be here to hear it. If I may?

**Allworthy** Very well.

**Mrs Waters** Tom, please will you come in?

**Tom** *enters*.

**Allworthy** Tom.

**Tom** Mr Allworthy – your servant. Mr Weston. Sophia.

**Allworthy** Madam, may I ask why is it that you think I planned to prosecute Tom?

**Mrs Waters** Yesterday I had a visit from a gentleman who, taking me for Fitzpatrick's wife, said that if Mr Jones had murdered my husband I would be provided with finances to persecute the case. I enquired of this gentleman his name but he would not avail me of it, but luckily I already knew it. It was none other than Mr Blifil.

**Allworthy**　Blifil?

**Mrs Waters**　Yes, sir. I assumed he was acting on your behalf.

**Allworthy**　Why no.

**Blifil**　The woman is lying, sir.

**Mrs Waters**　What reason would I have to lie?

**Allworthy**　I know not, madam, but I do not make the habit of believing such accusations from someone I have just met, especially when they are made against a person of my own family.

**Mrs Waters**　It has been so long that I see you do not recollect me.

**Allworthy**　Have we met before?

**Mrs Waters**　Indeed, for before I married my husband, Captain Waters, my name was Jones – Jenny Jones.

**Weston**　Jenny Jones!

**Tom**　Jenny Jones?

**Sophia**　Tom's mother.

**Tom**　My mother?

**Allworthy**　Why, madam, this is indeed a surprise.

**Tom**　But didn't we . . . oh, my God.

**Allworthy**　If you had not acquainted me of your identity I should have never had guessed it.

**Tom**　I don't feel well.

**Mrs Waters**　Do you remember, sir, a young man whose name was Summer?

**Allworthy**   Yes, of course I do, he was a good friend of mine. A young man of great learning and virtue. I maintained him at university and after his studies he came to reside at the house.

**Mrs Waters**   Yes, a fine man; genteel and handsome with so much wit and good breeding. It was a sad loss when he died so young.

**Allworthy**   Yes, he was untimely snatched away, but little did I think he had any sins of this kind to answer for, for I plainly perceive you are going to tell me that he is the father of your child.

**Mrs Waters**   Indeed, sir, he was not. He was the father of this child, but not by me.

**Tom**   You're not my mother?

**Mrs Waters**   No.

**Tom**   Oh, thank God.

**Allworthy**   But you yourself confessed it to me.

**Mrs Waters**   So far what I confessed was true. That these hands carried the infant to your bed. I conveyed it there on the command of the mother. And afterwards owned it, and thought myself by herself generously rewarded for both my secrecy and shame.

**Allworthy**   Who could this woman be?

**Mrs Waters**   Indeed I tremble to name her.

**Allworthy**   By all this preparation I am to guess she is a relation of mine.

**Mrs Waters**   Indeed she was a near one. It was your sister, sir.

**Allworthy**   Can it be possible?

**Mrs Waters**   My mother and myself did only attend at the birth. You were away in London, sir, and, on the instructions

of your sister, I laid the infant on your bed, for she knew
your nature and that you would bring the boy up as one of
your own. Thus you have at last discovered your nephew.

**Tom**   My uncle.

**Allworthy**   My nephew. It is strange, I find it hard to
believe but I know it is true. But how can my sister have
taken this secret with her to the grave?

**Mrs Waters**   She did not. I was with her in the last days. I
wrote the letter for her as she dictated it, informing you of
what I have just told you. It is not until recently that I have
discovered that you did not receive it.

**Allworthy**   What happened to it?

**Mrs Waters**   The man who delivered it put it into the hands
of Mr Blifil.

**Blifil**   This is ridiculous, Uncle . . .

**Allworthy**   Enough. I have heard enough. Now, sir, before
you pack your bags and get out of my sight do find that
letter your mother sent me.

**Blifil**   But Uncle . . .

**Allworthy**   No buts, sir, I will no longer listen to your lies.
Now get out of my sight I can no longer look upon you. You
are no longer welcome here, sir, and in the morning I will
call my lawyer and have you struck from my will.

**Blifil**   Uncle.

**Allworthy**   Go! (**Blifil** *exits*.) What amends can I ever make
to you for those unkind and unjust suspicions that I have
entertained, and for all the sufferings that I have occasioned
you?

**Tom**   It is amends enough, sir, to call you uncle.

**Allworthy**   And Mrs Waters, how can I ever thank you?

**Mrs Waters**   To see young Tom restored once more to his
family is reward enough, sir.

**Weston**   What the bloody hell is going on here Allworthy?

**Allworthy**   It looks as if, dear neighbour, I will not be able to honour our contract.

**Weston**   Well, that's all fine then isn't it.

**Allworthy**   That is as it stands.

**Weston**   What do you mean?

**Allworthy**   Well, your daughter obviously cannot marry Master Blifil.

**Weston**   Cannot marry Blifil?

**Allworthy**   No, but I do have a near relation who I know has the totally opposite character to the wretch, and of whose fortune I am prepared to make equal.

**Weston**   Really?

**Allworthy**   Yes.

**Weston**   Who's that then?

**Allworthy**   Why Tom of course.

**Weston**   Jones?

**Allworthy**   What do you say Miss Weston?

**Sophia**   I am truly sorry, sir, but I could not accept Mr Jones as my husband.

**Allworthy**   But I thought that you were inclined to Mr Jones.

**Sophia**   I might be, sir, but I cannot marry against my father's wishes.

**Weston**   Now hang on a moment, hang on. Let's not be hasty. Now, have I got this right. Jones is your nephew, Blifil has been kicked out on his ear, and you are going to give Jones Blifil's fortune and make him your heir?

**Allworthy**   That is correct, neighbour.

**Weston**   Sophy, what is all this? You know I have loved Tom like my own son, nothing would make me happier than to see you two married.

**Sophia**   But Father . . .

**Weston**   No, Sophy, I am resolved to it. (*Turning to* **Tom**.) My old friend Tom. All past must be forgotten, where a body means no harm, what signifies a hasty word or two? One Christian should forgive and forget another.

**Tom**   I hope, sir, I shall never forget any obligations I have had to you, but as to any offence to me I declare I am an utter stranger.

**Weston**   I swear there ain't a hearty or more honest cock in all the kingdom. (*Taking him to* **Sophia** *and placing her hand in his*.) There we are my little honeys. Well what shall it be, tomorrow or the next day? It shan't be put off a minute longer than the next day, I am resolved to it.

**Tom**   Let me beseech you, sir . . .

**Weston**   Beseech, my arse. I thought thou had'st been a lad of higher mettle than to give way to a parcel of maidenish tricks. She'd have you tonight with all her heart, would'st not Sophy? Come confess, be an honest girl for once. What, art dumb? Why dost not speak?

**Sophia**   Why should I confess, sir, when you are so well acquainted with my thoughts.

**Weston**   That's a good girl. Doth consent then?

**Sophia**   No, indeed sir, I have given no such consent.

**Sophia** *her hand away from* **Tom**.

**Weston**   And won't have him then, not tomorrow or the next day?

**Sophia**   Indeed sir, I have no such intention.

**Weston**   What? First you wants him then you don't. You're all the spirit of contrary, and I know why. It's because you loves to be disobedient and to plague and vex thy father.

**Tom**   Pray, sir . . .

**Weston** (*To* **Tom**.)   I'll tell thee she art a puppy. When I forbade thee there was nothing but sighing and whining, now I am for thee she's against thee.

**Sophia**   What would my papa have me do?

**Weston**   What would I have thee do? Why give him yer hand this moment.

**Sophia**   Well, sir, I will obey. Here is my hand Mr Jones.

**Weston**   Well? Will you consent to have him tomorrow morning?

**Sophia**   I will be obedient to you, sir.

**Weston**   Why then, tomorrow shall be the day?

**Sophia**   Why then, tomorrow shall be the day, papa, since you have it so.

**Allworthy**   Nephew, I felicitate you most heartily, for I think you are the happiest of men.

**Weston**   Allworthy, I'll wager thee five pound to a crown we have a boy tomorrow nine months. Come neighbour, a drink to seal the contract.

**Weston** *and* **Allworthy** *exit.*

**Tom**   Sophia.

**Sophia**   Tom.

*They kiss.*

**Fielding** *enters.*

**Fielding**   And so ends our feast. Mr Allworthy hath never yet prevailed upon to see Blifil, but he had yielded to the importunity of Tom and Sophia to settle £200 a year upon him, which Blifil used to buy himself a seat in Parliament. Mr Thwackam married the voluptuous Molly and they have nearly a dozen children – none of them his. Mrs Fitzpatrick was separated from her husband and retained what was left of her fortune. Mrs Weston was reconciled with her niece and she and Lady Bellaston, who treated Tom in their first public meeting as a complete stranger, visit the happy couple frequently – much to the happy couple's annoyance. Squire Weston resigned his family seat and the greater part of his estate to his son-in-law and retired to a lesser house, which is more convenient for hunting and where he can get drunk to his heart's content and entertain who he likes. Sophia produced two fine children, a boy and a girl, of whom Squire Weston and Mr Allworthy are both delighted. Mint anyone?

For a complete listing of
Methuen Drama titles, visit:
**www.bloomsbury.com/drama**

Follow us on Twitter and keep up to date
with our news and publications
**@MethuenDrama**